"Michelle McKinney Hammond has a unique way of bringing the characters of Scripture to life in a real and practical way. At times I see myself in her words, at times others, but always I see the sovereignty of God directing and guiding behind the scenes. Michelle makes Scripture applicable to today's problems, so that we soon discover they are not all that unique after all."

—GIGI GRAHAM TCHIVIDJIAN, speaker and author
of *A Quiet Knowing* and *Weatherproof Your Heart*

"The rich, down-to-earth, simple yet profound stories in this powerful book help us open our eyes to the sources, resources, and strategies of dealing with everyday life.... When you read this book with your eyes open and your heart ready to live the abundant life promised by Jesus, you will be able to see inside yourself. Then you'll see that looking up to Jesus, the source of your strength, will be so much easier."

—THELMA WELLS, speaker and author
of *Girl, Have I Got Good News for You!*
and *Bumblebees Fly Anyway: Defying The Odds*
at Work and Home

"*Get Over It And On With It* is truly empowering. Each and every chapter is personal, practical, and applicable. On the one hand I hear the voice of experience; on the other, I hear the voice of a girlfriend. Either way, because Michelle's love for the Word of God is so evident, there's no way one can miss hearing the voice of God."

—BABBIE MASON, author and Christian singer/songwriter

GET OVER IT

and

ON WITH IT!

GET OVER IT

and

ON WITH IT!

HOW *to* GET UP WHEN
LIFE KNOCKS YOU DOWN

MICHELLE McKINNEY HAMMOND

WATERBROOK
PRESS

GET OVER IT AND ON WITH IT!
PUBLISHED BY WATERBROOK PRESS
2375 Telstar Drive, Suite 160
Colorado Springs, Colorado 80920
A division of Random House, Inc.

ISBN 1-57856-450-6

Published in association with the literary agency of Alive Communications, Inc., 7680 Goddard Street, Suite 200, Colorado Springs, CO 80920.

Printed in the United States of America

This is for those who are dismayed,
resigned,
in wonderment,
or simply hurting
from the fresh wounds that life has inflicted.

➤ ➤ ➤

There is hope.
And the knowledge of this truth is merely the beginning…

CONTENTS

Foreword by Dr. Luther J. Blackwell Jr. xiii

Acknowledgments xv

Introduction: What Is It About Life? 1

When Life Knocks the Wind Out of You 9

PART I: ABSORBING THE BLOW 13

   1. Rest 15

   2. Eat 19

   3. Drink 22

   4. Build Your House 26

   5. Run for Cover 31

   6. Climb Higher 34

   7. Get in the Spirit 37

When Life Assaults Your Faith 43

PART II: GETTING YOUR SECOND WIND 45

   8. Get Real 47

   9. Don't Just Lay There! Wrestle! 52

  10. Seek the True Solution 56

  11. Get Help 60

  12. Discard Negative Advice 66

  13. Don't Ask Why, Ask What 70

  14. Leave Your Defense to God 74

  15. Understand the Season 78

  16. Wait It Out 83

When Life Destroys Your Dreams 87

PART III: GETTING BACK ON YOUR FEET 89
  17. Keep Your Head Above Water 91
  18. Lay Aside the Former Glory 94
  19. Let Go of What You're Used To 98
  20. Be Excellent No Matter What! 101
  21. Maintain Your Integrity 104
  22. Fight the Urge to Blame 107
  23. Remain Gracious 110

When Life Robs Your Peace 115

PART IV: STANDING FIRM 117
  24. Remember Who You Are 119
  25. Be Resourceful 123
  26. Stand in the Gap 126
  27. Pick Your Battles 130
  28. Leave the Rest to God 134

When Life Takes What Is Dear 139

PART V: LETTING GO AND MOVING FORWARD 143
  29. Know When It's Over 145
  30. Keep the Good Parts 150
  31. Love Those Who Are Available to Be Loved 153
  32. Be Prepared for Change 157
  33. Bank on the Future 160
  34. Let Go of the Idols 163
  35. Get Over It 168
  36. Learn Your Lesson 172

37. Walk, Don't Run 175
38. Face Your Fears................................. 178
39. Be Open....................................... 182
40. Do What You've Never Done Before 187
41. Release the Unknown........................... 192

When Life Hits Home 197

PART VI: GETTING ON WITH IT 201
42. Release Your Captors 203
43. Don't Just Bloom! Flourish! 209
44. Fight Your Real Enemy.......................... 214

Afterword: Stay Ahead of the Game........................ 217
Bible Characters Referenced in This Book.................. 223

Foreword

Michelle McKinney Hammond is one of the most exuberant and effervescent young women I have met in my fifty years of ministry. Not only do these words characterize her, but consistency, focus, and durability are also her strengths. I have watched her grapple with life in its disappointing seasons, only to see her emerge with the smell of victory permeating her personality.

It is difficult to go through life's ups and downs and not gain insight. *Get Over It and On With It!* is a wonderful manual on how Michelle herself has successfully handled life's struggles and won. It is a guide for success, simply because it is Scripturally based and sound in the manner in which God charts our pathways.

Along with the aforementioned, the book has personality! You will laugh, cry, think, and ultimately rejoice as you come to understand that you can leap every hurdle thrown across your path. You will be brought to a wonderful realization that *getting over* means "sailing above," and *getting on* means leaving those things behind you while living in a brighter hope. You will conclude the reading of this book by saying, "There really is gain in my pain, promotion in the commotion, and advances in all circumstances."

Dr. Luther J. Blackwell Jr.
Senior Pastor, Mega Church
Cleveland, Ohio

ACKNOWLEDGMENTS

To my dear parents and siblings, including the in-laws: I not only love you, but I really like you, adore you, and treasure you... You are my fortress. Thanks for keeping me surrounded with your love.

Well, what can I say? Thank you Dan Rich for making an investment in my growth. Truly life stretches us—ah, but what we reach makes the struggle worth it. Erin Healy, my beloved editor, you worked hard for the money this time, girl (ha, ha)! You make my work a pleasure. I thank God for you.

To the WaterBrook family: Don, Laura, Kirsten, the sales staff, and all those (mentioned and unmentioned) who work so hard on my behalf. You are loved and appreciated. You'd better know that! Laura Wright, thank you for catching everything I overlook and for asking all the right questions. You are on it, girl.

To my Bible study group: Ladies, as iron sharpens iron, you keep me on my p's and q's. I love you. Thank you for being there for me and allowing me to experiment on you.

To my "sister disciples," who have watched life happen to me over the years, dried my tears, and made me get up again: Brenda, Michelle, Theresa, Karen, Cindy, Jan, Charlotte, Nancy, Sheila, Dee Dee, Bunny, and Terri. Thank you for holding up my arms.

Peggy, thanks for listening late at night and for always making me smile when I would rather frown. Valencia, thanks for always having my back—God's gonna bless ya!

Chip McGregor, have I told you lately how much I appreciate you?

Once upon a time, there were twin brothers. One optimistic. One pessimistic. For the sake of understanding their different temperaments, their mother enlisted the help of a noted psychologist.

The psychologist instructed her to put the pessimistic child in a room filled with various sizes and shapes of wrapped presents. The optimistic child was to be placed in a room filled with manure.

With this task done, the mother and the psychologist visited the children to gauge each one's response to his circumstances. They found the pessimistic child sitting among his presents, gazing at them in complete disbelief. When asked why he had not opened any, he simply stated, "They couldn't possibly be for me!"

Moving on to the next child, they were a bit concerned to see no sign of him in the manure-filled room. They called for him, and his head emerged from one of the piles. When asked what he was doing, he answered, "With this much mess, there's got to be a pony in here somewhere!"

—Author Unknown

WHAT IS IT ABOUT LIFE?

"A funny thing happened on my way to a perfectly fabulous life…"

People have stories. You could probably contribute a few of your own. Good ones. Bad ones. Happy ones. Sad ones. Pretty ones. Ugly ones. Stories of love, betrayal, hopes, failure, and all the in-between. Stories that describe one fellow we all know: *life*.

➤ ➤ ➤

"Oh, I definitely had a different picture of how my life was supposed to go," she said, looking weary from her disappointment. "I thought I was on the right track. According to my schedule, I would arrive in the land of 'married-happily-ever-after' by twenty-five. I would have my first child at twenty-seven, the second at twenty-nine. We'd accumulate the house, two-car garage, one luxury vehicle, one family car, and a cute dog by thirty-five. And by fifty-five I would be free to retire and live my life going on cruises with my husband. Nice and tidy. No drama. But somewhere along the way I must have turned left instead of right." A wry smile. "Well, now I'm kissing forty. Still single. Life hasn't exactly worked out the way I planned."

➤ ➤ ➤

He looked mildly surprised. "I was doing it! Flying in the big league. Producing some of the top acts in the country. My road was paved for continued success. I thought the deals and money would never end. Perhaps I was driving too fast and didn't see the bump coming. When I hit it, I felt it. But it was too late to recover. Bad decisions, bad business deals, bad women…they all caught up with me. Now I'm starting over. I don't even have a place to live. I'm talking starting from scratch. That's my story. I should be much farther along than I am, and to tell you the truth, I feel stuck. I've got to get it together. But I just don't know how."

❧ ❧ ❧

"We had a wonderful courtship, an incredible wedding. Life was good. With the pending birth of our first child, I felt we were well on our way. Then my wife died in childbirth. I don't know what to say. I'm so filled with grief I feel I will die myself. I'm grieving the loss of my best friend, my wife, the mother of my child. I'm grieving for my daughter who will never experience how wonderful her mother was. I know life goes on, but how?"

❧ ❧ ❧

"My husband was a brilliant, gifted man with an incredible career. He suffered a massive stroke. He was only forty-seven with no history of bad health. Now his gifts are gone. He's learning to speak again. We're set financially, but I agonize over how he feels trapped inside of himself, unable to communicate even simple things. He is not the type to embrace helplessness. What does a man do with the rest of his life after something like this happens?"

❧ ❧ ❧

"I don't understand it. My son never hurt anyone; he was a fine young man. He graduated with honors, a scholarship, and the promise of a brilliant future. Why him? Why should he be gunned down senselessly by strangers driving by? He was on his way home!"

❧ ❧ ❧

"But my husband was a Christian. Christian men don't run off with their secretaries…"

"There has never been a history of cancer in my family. I eat right,

I exercise, I've taken better care of my body than most! How could this happen to me?"

"What do you do when everything you've worked for goes up in smoke?"

"I went from my father's house to my husband's house. I thought I would be married for the rest of my life. I'm afraid. I don't know how to adjust to life alone…"

THE WAY HOME

Ah, life. Wonderful! Terrible. Exhilarating! Terrifying. Beautiful! Ugly. Generous. Demanding. Fair. Unfair. Fulfilling. Draining. Rewarding. Disappointing. And relentless. We can all think of a lot of words to describe life based on our individual experiences, but I'm sure we can agree on at least one adjective: unpredictable. Let's face it. Life never goes as planned. For those of us who don't have a deliberate outline of the future, most of us generally have a subconscious expectation that at the very least, life will proceed undisturbed by major drama and interruptions. But this is rarely the case.

Is an uncomplicated life too much to hope for?

"Why not?" we demand. "I had all my pretty little ducks lined up in a row, and now look at them. Scattered to high heaven." Someone once said, "Man makes plans and God laughs." So whose fault is it when things don't go as scheduled? Is it our fault? God's fault? The devil's fault? Are we merely the haphazard victims of fate? Does life shoot random bullets, scatter our affairs, and then laugh hysterically as we dash about, desperately attempting to recover the pieces? How can you gain control of a life that is supposed to be yours but behaves as anything but that? *How does one catch a runaway train?* might be an easier question to answer, but I'll try the tougher one anyway.

How much power do we have over our own lives, really? Is absolutely *everything* up to God? To other powers that be? Who gets the first or the last say? What is our part in the movie of life? Do we have any say-so in the plot or the ending? Of course we do! Perhaps it's safe to say that when man makes plans *on his own,* God laughs. Not out of cruelty, but rather a rueful wish that He had been consulted. After all, He knows the full course of our lives, from beginning to end, while we merely see our history and our present desires.

In light of our limited insight, the inevitable is sure to happen. We hit a snag and get stuck. We find ourselves unable to move past our shock, our disappointment, or our own lack of knowing what to do next. Welcome to the real world, be you Christian or not. There is no yellow brick road. No Utopia. What we think will solve our problems usually doesn't. We, like Dorothy in *The Wizard of Oz,* discover the wizard is not who we thought he was.

Everyone we meet on the way to the fulfillment of our dreams is simply trying to do the same thing—get home. Home to the heart of our deepest desires. Home to a peaceful, settled life. Is it possible to find the way? By the grace of God and with the assistance of biblical wisdom, the answer is a resounding yes. Yes, if you are willing to look *up* instead of straight ahead. Yes, if you are willing to do the work to get past your present circumstances. Are you? Wouldn't you like to do more than just survive when life knocks you down? Wouldn't you like to thrive and emerge better for each trial you've endured? Before you answer too quickly, keep reading.

Over the course of this book, we'll spend some time with several men and women of the Bible. Very real men and women to whom life dealt very real troubles, just like yours. These men and women were every bit as human as you and I are; however, they figured out how to get up when life had seemingly leveled them to the ground. We can learn a great deal from each of them. I'm going to highlight portions of their various difficulties, but hang in there with me. Collectively, their stories of how they dealt with the broken pieces of their lives paint the big picture of how we can overcome.

For those of you who don't generally turn to the Bible for guidance in life's decisions, I ask you to bear with me. If you are reading this book, I will presume that you haven't yet found what you're looking for in your search for the solution to life's problems. You need to know that it is all right to admit that life is bigger than you are. Therefore, you need someone greater than yourself to deal with the circumstances in your life that seem humanly impossible to handle. Someone once said the Bible stands for Basic Instructions for living Before Leaving Earth. The bottom line is that the principles it offers us just make good sense. So keep an open mind. The beauty of scriptural principles is they work—whether you believe them or not!

DECISIONS, DECISIONS

Thomas la Mance once said, "Life is what happens to us while we are making other plans." Yet, contrary to that popular belief, life *doesn't* just happen. Choices happen. Decisions happen. A word said or not said. A deed done or not done. A moment seized or ignored. Life doesn't happen without our participation. Generally speaking, we pretty much get out of the pot what we put in it.

In the midst of this admittedly pat theory are instances when bad things happen to good people. When victims are innocent and random acts affect the undeserving. Such events cannot and will not be explained until the end of time when we all finally behold the entire picture. But even in these cases, if we could get the behind-the-scenes story, we would probably discover a multitude of circumstances converging into the major event. So many dominoes fall before the final one does. So many choices affect countless other people who were never part of the initial decisions.

Someone once asked me where God was when I was struck down by a truck on the street one day, leaving me with a permanently injured leg. Believe me, sustaining such an injury was not a part of my plan! I paused for a moment, thought about the events leading up to that incident, and answered with a laugh, "Probably in the same place He was when He tried to get me to cross the street at another spot." Actually, I believe He moved closer to hold me in the midst of my suffering. But I clearly recall that life-changing morning. As I strolled down the street, I felt an urging deep within to cross the street before I got to the corner. I argued with "myself" that I would have to walk through slush if I took that course of action. So I proceeded to the corner. Well, the rest is history.

God's Spirit longs to communicate with ours. To warn, advise, encourage, and inform us in the midst of every daily undertaking. Yes, in more cases than not, our calamities could be avoided if we would remain sensitive to the voice of God. Sometimes God doesn't have to warn us. Life itself warns us, throwing up little red flags along the way as we race toward a faulty decision. Whatever the source of caution, we often pause after the fact and reflect, "Something told me not to do that..." Does everyone receive warning of impending calamities? I think it's safe to say absolutely not. But I would venture to say we generally receive more warnings than we heed. Sad to say, but in a lot of cases, "A man's own folly ruins his life, yet his heart rages against the LORD" (Proverbs 19:3).

Whether we are active culprits or innocent bystanders, why does God allow misfortune to occur? Is there a purpose for all the suffering? We will wrestle with such questions from here to eternity. For now I will simply second the motion of another who said that God can turn what was meant for evil into good. "You intended to harm me," he told the men who had wronged him, "but God intended it for good to accomplish what is now being done" (Genesis 50:20). God does not delight in seeing us groan beneath the weight of our struggles, but I believe He uses our troubles to strengthen our character and ultimately position us to receive greater blessings. That is, if we let Him. It is still very much up to us to claim the best of what is left from a life that has not gone right by our estimations.

Picture this. It's the Olympics. Not the summer, not the winter—this is the lifetime Olympics. The event is the pole vault. You are the contender. Holding your pole, you stand ready to run. The gun sounds and you are off, measuring your steps. You dig the pole into the ground, sail through the air over the vault, and land in a cloud of glory. You made it! You cleared the barrier that could have halted your flight.

That pole is your pain, your disappointment, your fears. You can either drop it, carry it around, or use it to propel you to the next level of living. I urge you to grab it, hold it firmly, dig in, and use it to push you over your own doubts, the misunderstanding of others, the lack of cooperation from all who promised to rescue you, even your disgruntlement with life in general. With God. Perhaps with yourself. The choice is yours.

We have been deceived into believing that life has *us*. No, my friend, the truth of the matter is that *we* have life. Jesus said, "I have come that they may have life, and that they may have it more abundantly" (John 10:10, NKJV). How do we cash in on that promise of abundant living, especially when it seems life has gotten away from us? By making the right choices after we've been disappointed, that's how.

Now is not the time to lie down and roll over, to resign, or to give up the ship. Stop, yes. Evaluate, yes. Lay out a game plan, yes. But quit? Absolutely not! As we take the time to learn from the examples of a few major overcomers, it is my prayer that you will be able to adopt some sound and practical principles to see you through to the other side of your own situation. The fat lady hasn't sung yet; therefore, there is hope if you know where to turn!

WHEN LIFE KNOCKS
THE WIND OUT OF YOU

He was a real mover and shaker. A superpower. Rolling high in the political field. When he spoke, the world listened. His power was uncontested among those who admired him as well as those who inwardly seethed against him. All that he owned was protected, and he assumed that his reputation would guarantee his peace. Although he lived in a troubled time—the world suffered from economic crisis, drought, famine, and the lack of essentials for survival—he miraculously thrived, and all his needs were met.

But trouble was afoot. Terrorists arose and wiped out many of his governing colleagues. The rest went into hiding, fearing for their lives. In retaliation he cut off water supplies to the area that harbored his enemies. Confident that they had been bowed, he presented himself to their leader to try to talk reason into them.

But his enemy remained steadfastly opposed. So a summit was held to establish who would reign. They were no match for this great man, who called down fiery missiles and totally dismantled their base of power. In the aftermath of this display, their governing body was wiped out. His superiority proven, he reopened their water supply. But the wounded enemy was not to be appeased. They threatened personal retaliation, and he became gripped with fear. Forgetting his incredible victory, he fled for his life and plummeted into a paralyzing depression.

Though this story holds echoes of events triggered on September 11, 2001, these events of long ago are recorded in the book of 1 Kings, chapter 18. The man: the prophet Elijah. In that day, most of the prophets of the Lord had been slaughtered by order of the evil king Ahab and his even more evil wife, Jezebel. But Elijah did not walk in fear. He knew whom he served: the mighty God who would back him up. His prophetic gift was so powerful he was able to declare with confidence that there would be no rain in the land until he said so. And it was so. To the dismay of all, drought covered the land. When Ahab and Jezebel still refused to concede, Elijah challenged the prophets of Baal and invited them to prove the power of their god. Needless to say, Baal never showed up or performed on their behalf, but God did. Manifesting Himself as fire from the heavens, He consumed the waterlogged offerings that had been set before Him.

After making his point about God's superiority, Elijah ordered the prophets of Baal to be killed. All 450 of them. Queen Jezebel was none too happy to lose all of her lackeys in one day. So even though Elijah possessed the supernatural power to run ahead of Ahab's chariots, his confidence dwindled in the face of her deadly threats. Once on the mountaintop witnessing the power of God Almighty, he soon found himself in a dry place under a tree professing his weariness and praying for God to send death to save him from his misery.

When we are riding high, it is hard to fathom a low time in our lives. But when our personal security is threatened, weariness puts us at risk of casting down all that we know, of forgetting our former victories. Panic sets in and drains us not only of our confidence but also of the will to trust in God, to fight, and to believe that we will make it through. And yet we must move on with the business of life.

Danger is always present, threatening our family life, our financial security, and our personal well-being. When the rigors of life wear down our resistance to worry and fear, our will to continue is weakened. It is hard to discern what we should do next. Our seeming lack of control over the setbacks we experience causes us to become overwhelmed with resignation and apathy. God will not leave us in this place, although He will graciously allow us to entertain the reality of our feelings for a season.

How did Elijah bounce back from this experience? Indeed he did, but not without going through some necessary paces of restoration. We must take ourselves through the same steps when we find ourselves on this familiar ground. There is hope for those who feel they have no defense against circumstances that threaten what they hold dear. But there is work to be done in order to get back up to the mountaintop where the air is clear. The steps I'll outline in Part I may seem simplistic, yet they are profound and often overlooked as we scramble to pick up the pieces of our lives. No, your future has not been shattered, just rearranged in order to prepare a better way for you.

PART I

ABSORBING THE BLOW

Myth
Life should go the way we want it to.

❧ ❧ ❧

Truth
These things I have spoken to you, that in Me you may
have peace. In the world you will have tribulation; but be of
good cheer, I have overcome the world.

JOHN 16:33, NKJV

REST

You might be thinking, *Now is not the time to rest, Michelle. I've been stagnant long enough.* So you've been lethargic. Not doing much of anything and caring even less. It's all right. Let yourself go there for now. I find it interesting that God didn't confront Elijah about his lack of faith at this time. Perhaps He knew something Elijah didn't. In fact, I *know* He did. God realizes that we are merely puffed-up dust, as a friend of mine so simply puts it. "He knows how we are formed, he remembers that we are dust" (Psalm 103:14). He knows that in our humanity we can only take so much. Therefore, He who designed and created us knows that if we keep pushing ourselves, we will eventually run out of steam.

Depression is not simply emotional; it can be physiological as well. I like to think of our systems as being housed around a fuse box much like the boxes in our homes. When the circuits of our physical body and our emotions become overloaded, our system shuts down to keep us from blowing up. In our panic, we sometimes beat ourselves into getting up and running again before we're ready. Fortunately, our system refuses to cooperate until everything within us has had the time it needs to cool down. The body takes over and refuses to generate the energy needed to keep up our former pace. It even refuses the normal amount of food we usually eat because of the work involved in processing it. At the bottom line, our body simply says, "Time out! I need to stop and regroup."

Now is not the time to be impatient with yourself. Listen to your body and let it recover. Don't push it. Take it one day at a time. Allow yourself to grow stronger gradually.

As Elijah lay under that tree complaining about his lot in life, the Lord allowed him to sleep—for a time. God didn't have a problem with that. You see, "There remains, then, a Sabbath-rest for the people of God.... Let us, therefore, make every effort to enter that rest..." (Hebrews 4:9,11). How can we rest and exert effort at the same time? The only effort necessary is making the decision to stop everything. This has to be an active decision for most of us who are driven by the compulsion to constantly be "doing" something. It is hard for us to simply "be." Be where we are. Be who we are. Be still. Simply be. When you can no longer "do" anything, be still and know that He is God. He will take care of what you cannot. God is not of the opinion—as most of Western culture is—that we are validated by what we do.

God is serious about rest. As a matter of fact, He *insists* that we rest. Rest energizes us to produce greater things in our lives. It gives us a second wind and restores our strength. This is why He makes a very specific promise to us concerning rest:

> If you keep your feet from breaking the Sabbath
> and from doing as you please on my holy day,
> if you call the Sabbath a delight
> and the LORD's holy day honorable,
> and if you honor it by not going your own way
> and not doing as you please or speaking idle words,
> then you will find your joy in the LORD,
> and I will cause you to ride on the heights of the land
> and to feast on the inheritance of your father Jacob.
> (Isaiah 58:13-14)

What was the inheritance of Jacob? The legacy of a strong and enduring family lineage as well as wealth and honor. These blessings are the result of right priorities, of taking the time to invest in what is truly important in life. When we are caught up in a constant whirlwind of activity, our priorities slip, and we lose our grasp of the important things.

Remember when everything was closed on Sundays? Families *had* to spend time together. It was a day for church, dinner together, and rest.

Families talked and shared what was on their hearts. It was the day of preparation for the upcoming week. Those who rested and prepared were revitalized, ready to face Monday when it rolled around. Now we are just as busy on Sunday as we are any other day of the week. Oh sure, some of us stop by to visit God on the way to all the other things on our agenda for the day. Small wonder we are burned out. Still exhausted when Monday comes, wondering how we will make it to Friday. Exhaustion takes its toll. We are too weary to give our all and perform with excellence. Our minds and senses are not as sharp. We miss important cues at home as well as at work.

Then one day we wake up and wonder what happened to our world. When did the downward slide begin? When did my child get ensnared with the wrong friends? When did my mate's eyes begin to wander? How could I have overlooked that pile of paperwork? How could I have let things get so out of hand? How could I have missed it?

We "miss it" because we are too busy—and too tired—to notice.

But God says if we obey His command, if we give the Sabbath to Him, He will rejuvenate us as we bask in His presence. We will be equipped to be on top of the world. We will be filled with joy because we will not be worn out, and that joy will be translated into quick wits that will bring you favor. Our relationships will work better because we will feel and be more pleasant. We will prosper on all fronts because our strength won't be sapped. We will have nowhere to go but up. Up to the place of wealth and honor, spiritually, physically, and emotionally.

What happens when you refuse to rest? Well, you can count on the opposite of all the goodies mentioned above. In short, life itself will force you to rest eventually. You will run out of steam and land in the bondage of your own depletion. Consider the children of Israel who refused to stop planting crops for 490 years in a row, though God had asked them to let the land rest every seven years. They ended up in bondage in Babylon for exactly seventy years. Let's see: 490 divided by seven equals exactly seventy. That land got the rest it needed. Funny how things have a way of catching up with us. You will rest whether you like it or not. Wouldn't you prefer it to be your choice?

Although Elijah was very dramatic about his feelings, he realized his need for rest and did not resist either his body or God's instruction. He let rest do its work. Yes, he had wielded great power at one time, but for now he had done enough.

When you've come to the end of your road and carried one heavy burden too many, truly it is time to stop and rest.

➤ LOOKING INWARD ◄

- What happens to your present problem when you bury yourself in distracting activities?
- What keeps you from resting?
- What are you afraid to hear if you stop to rest?
- Do you associate resting with failure or being out of control? If so, why?
- What do you think will happen if you stop trying to make things happen? Will things change if you don't?
- Do you trust God to handle things? Why or why not?

➤ LOOKING UPWARD ◄

"This is what the Sovereign LORD, the Holy One of Israel, says: 'In repentance and rest is your salvation, in quietness and trust is your strength'" (Isaiah 30:15).

EAT

But I don't feel like eating, you say. As I mentioned in chapter 1, this is a natural response to exhaustion. But I am talking about a different kind of food here. What you eat at this time of your life is very important. What you digest will either build you up or weaken your system even more.

I recall being glued to the television almost twenty hours a day after the attacks on the World Trade Center. I was obsessed with and consumed by the events. Who was responsible? What would be done? Had any victims been found alive? What did all of this mean for the days to come? I found I couldn't carry out daily tasks, so bound was I by worry. Could I ever get on a plane again? But a sudden thought broke through the doom and gloom I had become so deeply entrenched in. "Faith comes by hearing…"

Yikes! If I was only hearing despair and fear, I wouldn't have a ray of hope left to cling to. I had to make a decision. Even though I feared missing important news, I had to turn off my television set and clear my mind. I limited myself to one hour of updates in the evening. My fear began to diminish, and my energy returned. I began to function again, praying for those who had been affected and trusting God to keep me safe and to restore order to the world.

In the battle of the flesh versus the spirit, whichever we feed the most will become the strongest. If we constantly feed ourselves fear, we will be consumed by anxiety. If we keep eating morsels of negativity, we will be overwhelmed with hopelessness. All of these inner attitudes will manifest themselves in our outward behaviors until we find ourselves reeling out of control. Ah, but if we feed ourselves positive thoughts, seeds of faith, then hope begins to burst through all the heaviness we feel. "Whatever is true, whatever is noble, whatever is right, whatever is pure…think about such things" (Philippians 4:8). Light will overtake the darkness in our psyche, and we will feel ourselves coming alive inside again.

God anticipated the fact that Elijah would be starving for reassurance that everything was going to be all right. So He sent an angel to wake the disillusioned prophet and instruct him to eat. The angel of the Lord prepared a cake of bread for him. This is significant. Why not meat? Why not vegetables? Why bread?

The bread is spiritually significant of the Word of God. Jesus is the Word of God in human flesh, the Bread of Life. We must consume and savor His promises. We need to digest not what everyone around us is saying about our problems, but what God has promised He will do in the midst of our emergencies. He has promised not to drop the ball. He has promised to be present and accounted for, to give us the power to overcome whatever we face. That truth is what we must feed ourselves. His words are what we must chew on until we have fully digested what He is saying, until those words become a part of us, until what God says about our situation drowns out every negative voice within us. His are words of life. Words of victory. Precious promises from One who cannot lie.

Yes, when we are starving for a grain of hope that will strengthen us to keep on keeping on in spite of what we see, how we feel, and what we fear, I can't think of a better time to eat.

➤ LOOKING INWARD ◄

- What has your spiritual and emotional diet consisted of lately?
- Have you been feeding your flesh or your spirit? Briefly describe your diet.
- What do you need to cut out of your diet?

- What do you need to work into your eating regimen?
- What small appetizer can you begin with? Which of God's promises fills you with strength for the days ahead?

➤ LOOKING UPWARD ◄

"He humbled you, causing you to hunger and then feeding you with manna, which neither you nor your fathers had known, to teach you that man does not live on bread alone but on every word that comes from the mouth of the LORD" (Deuteronomy 8:3).

3

DRINK

When you're thirsty, there is nothing like a cold drink. You can almost feel it going all the way down. Washing and cooling your insides. Refreshing you, making you feel new again. Yes, a drink is a powerful thing. The angel of the Lord who visited Elijah knew the power of a good drink of cleansing, healing water and made sure that Elijah was supplied with what he needed for resuscitation.

What is the first thing you generally offer a guest in your home? You got it! Something to drink. Why? Because you know instinctively that, even if you have nothing for them to eat, liquid will fill them. It is a way of not allowing them to remain empty in your presence. God could not bear for you to remain in His presence unfilled either. Water fills as no other substance can. It is able to fill any vacant shape. Noted Bible teacher Beth Moore illustrates this by putting symbols of all the things we try to stuff our lives with—money, toys, personal effects—into a vase. Even when chock-full, the vase is riddled with empty spaces. Then she takes water and pours it over the contents until the vase brims over. It is the water, not the things, that completes the filling process.

When Jesus sat at the well with the Samaritan woman (see John 4), He asked her to give Him a drink. But she couldn't. She was empty herself. Spiritually speaking, people generally don't have refreshing reserves to offer us not because they don't want to, but because they are overwhelmed by their own need. God alone can saturate the parched cracks and crevices of our souls. Jesus told the woman if she knew whom she was talking to and the gift that He wanted to give her (lasting fulfillment), *she* would ask *Him* for a drink. The water He had would satisfy her in such a way that she would never be thirsty again. What He had to offer her was a full measure of joy and an immovable peace that no one nor any circumstance could diminish. She wanted that water! We all want that water!

And that was the water God offered Elijah. An earthen vessel filled with water poured straight from the fountain of Living Water. There was nothing stagnant or lifeless about this water. It had the power to fill and then regenerate Elijah's inner man. It had the power to wash, heal, and restore. God did not rush Elijah's resuscitation. He was willing to give that weary man as much divine provision as he needed for strength to resume his life journey. God knew the pilgrimage would be too much for Elijah to endure without His help. So He let Elijah sleep and rest in His presence. The angel of the Lord woke him to feed and refresh him. He allowed him to sleep some more and then woke him to eat and drink again.

God's water is the knowledge of His presence in our lives, which gives us new hope and a new attitude based on what He has said in His Word. Accept His promises of being able to keep you through your difficult time, and keep drinking of His assurance until your thirst is satisfied.

When we're struggling to recover, we can only take a little at a time, but that is all right. One sip gives you enough to get you started. It's called process. Taking one step at a time. Allowing yourself to regroup bit by bit. The secret is to take one day at a time. It is all you can be held accountable for.

Allow the water that God gives to do all that it can do. First, the water of the Word will wash you and remove the residue of your bad experiences (see Ephesians 5:26). Then the Holy Spirit will unleash a river of life within you that will shoot up like a fountain and refill you. All that drained you of energy and hope will be submerged and will dissipate beneath its strong current, and the Holy Spirit will supply you with the refreshment you need.

Water is an incredible thing. Consider that the lack of it can snuff out the life of even the most powerful nation. Nothing can stop it if the boundaries built to hold it back collapse. It can be both destructive and beneficial. Storms can level crops and communities alike, but the soft rains of heaven can bring new life to dead places. The human body is made up of mostly water. Our spirit draws its life from the very breath of God. So why is it that we strain to live independently from the very things that make up the greater part of our being? Water is necessary. God is also necessary. We cannot live without either one.

Small wonder that one of Israel's greatest kings, David, compared his need for God to his need for water. "As the deer pants for streams of water, so my soul pants for you, O God" (Psalm 42:1).

Perhaps your thirst is a spiritual one. Perhaps you've tried to refresh yourself by drinking from the wrong fountains, fountains that offer no sustenance and eventually run dry. Perhaps it is time to partake of new fare. Elijah ate. You must eat. And then wash down what God tells you with His water. Some of the things we eat are harder to digest than others. They actually cause us to become thirsty. When we have difficulty swallowing, the natural inclination is to take a sip of something so that what we are eating will go down more easily.

Sometimes we have difficulty receiving all that God might be trying to tell us about our situation. But then He pours us a drink to help our spirit absorb what has been served. Drink in His presence and the refreshing relief it brings. He is the consummate host. He doesn't rush us through the meal. He simply makes what we need available to us and leaves us to partake of it at will. It is then up to us to take what is offered to strengthen ourselves. So don't just lie there, drink up.

➤ LOOKING INWARD ➤

- What do you thirst for right now?
- What or who has failed to satisfy you up to this point in your life?

- Have you tried to fill all the empty spaces in your life by your own efforts? What do you find still missing?
- What things do you need to be cleansed of in order to have a new start?
- What has blocked your ability to adapt to the changes in your life?

➤ LOOKING UPWARD ◄

"In the last day, that great day of the feast, Jesus stood and cried, saying, If any man thirst, let him come unto me, and drink." (John 7:37, KJV).

BUILD YOUR HOUSE

None of us really get to run from our troubles. We, like Elijah, are forced to rest and then face where we really live. After the Israelites were taken into captivity by the Babylonians—remember that seventy-year rest the land of Israel finally received?—the first thing God told them to do was to build houses on their captors' soil and dwell in them. I can imagine their reaction to His instruction: "What?! You mean we should set up shop in the middle of a situation we don't want to be in? We just want to get out of here!"

Perhaps your response would be similar if I told you to put down your roots right where you are. I hear you, I hear you, but let's just stop and think about this. Let's not look at "building your house" as the same thing as building a monument to your situation. Instead, let's consider this an opportunity to get your bearings so you can better deal with where you are. Though God told the Israelites to build physical houses, I am going to talk about building your spiritual house. This is a crucial task, because a strong house will be your only solid refuge in the midst of your ever-changing world.

Stop! Rest! Get nourishment! Take the time to stabilize yourself so you can think clearly. The first step one must take when building a house is to pick a desirable location. In a perfect world no one wants to build a house in a crowded area. We desire space and a good view. The same can be said of your spirit. It is hard to hear any voice of reason, let alone God's, if you are surrounded by clutter or in noisy surroundings. Select a place where you can settle yourself and get in touch with the peace God offers to you. He is not going to shout above the noise. He will not elbow His way through the advice of others. He will simply wait until you are in a space of quiet before He speaks. Whether it's the lakefront, a park bench, your favorite chair in the living room, your closet, your bathroom—wherever! Find a place to build your house and renew your spirit, then learn to settle there.

Next, prepare the foundation for the building. The foundation is the core of your belief system. Whatever you believe will shape your decisions and direct the course of your life. You will become what you believe. The bottom line? You really will live within the confines of the attitudes you nurture. If you think you are a failure, you will fail. If you believe you are undesirable, you will invite rejection. Where does your heart, your spirit, reside? That is where you truly live. And where you live influences the type of guests who visit you. Victory is not going anywhere near Failure's neighborhood. Therefore, carefully consider where you want to live by being honest with yourself about what you believe.

Now, I'm not talking about changing your life with some sort of positive-thinking mantra. No, I'm prodding you to deal with more important questions about the deep-seated beliefs of your heart. Who is God? Is He interested in your situation? Will He really come through? What does He have to say for Himself? What you believe about God will affect your reaction to any situation. The drowning man who believes no one will save him will flail frantically, thereby speeding up his demise. But the drowning man who sees that assistance is on the way will try to relax and keep himself afloat until his help arrives.

Do you believe that God exists? Do you believe that God is who He says He is? And that He will do what He says He will do? Yes or no? Satan targeted Job, causing him to lose everything—his children, his livestock, his property—to natural disaster and enemy attack. His own health deteriorated to the point that not even his wife wanted to be around him. She advised him to curse God and die. Yet Job clung to his only hope: "I know that my Redeemer lives" (Job 19:25). This sound belief was the house no one could destroy.

Once, after unexpectedly losing my job, I sat back to take stock of my situation. I had no savings and lots of financial obligations. My severance would be gone in no time. I had no prospects for another job anytime soon. A friend said to me, "Aren't you frantic?" My answer was "If someone told me that God had left the throne and gone on an indefinite sabbatical, then I would freak out. But as long as He is still in place, I'm not worried. I know He will take care of me." And He did.

Do you think God is unfair? sexist? narrow-minded? You must lay these issues to rest if you want your foundation to be solid. First, let's face it: Life is unfair, but God is just. Second, don't confuse machismo with God's heart. God is Spirit. Those who worship Him must do so from their spirits and then live out the truth of His Word. The title "Father" (though perhaps you have not had a positive experience with your earthly father) speaks of God's *position* as protector and provider in our lives, not of *gender*. Man and woman were both made in the image of God in order to glorify Him. Therefore, in the mind of God, both are powerful and necessary in order for the world to function at its best. As for narrow-mindedness, well, admit it: God is always right. Ever notice that successful people are narrow-minded? They don't allow anyone to sway them from their opinions or goals. We call them "focused." Open-mindedness leaves us open to too many distracting options that ultimately lead us away from what we truly desire. Man thinks a lot of things are right (*there's* a standard that constantly shifts!), but consider how many of our humanity-tainted choices propel us down the pathway toward death, the death of our dreams, our health, our relationships, and our overall well-being. "There is a way that seems right to a man," Scripture tells us, "but in the end it leads to death" (Proverbs 14:12).

Do you believe God blesses those who look for Him? Ahhh, this is where we might run into a bit of trouble. I don't think most of us have a problem believing God exists. But will He bless us? Now, that's a different subject. Especially if in your mind God hasn't shown up yet to give you some things that you want. Still, God requires that we believe He exists and that He rewards those who diligently seek Him (see Hebrews 11:6). If you don't believe this, I guarantee you will become like that drowning man. You'll begin to flail in your circumstances and, in most cases, will do more damage than good. So stop where you are. Make the choice to believe there is a God. Not only does He want to help, but He can. And better yet, He *will*.

So establish the fact that you are not alone. Build on that foundation. Don't erect walls around your heart, but do set healthy boundaries to ensure that you remain in sound mind and a quiet disposition. How do you do this? By allowing into your house only those people who will help you build it. The wrecking crew has already leveled whatever was standing before; don't invite a repeat occurrence. Guard what is precious—your heart. "Above all else, guard your heart" (Proverbs 4:23). Its condition is a matter of life and death.

Now paint your exterior. In the same way that what is in our heart shows up visibly in our life course, our outward demeanor can also affect our spirit. So get a new attitude. Attitude is half of what it takes to win the battle. Ever notice the posture of a woman who is dressed up versus one who goes casual? Her head is a little higher, her shoulders and back straighter. Her walk changes. Her demeanor and even the pitch of her voice are more mellow. The change attracts those who might have overlooked her before. Joy attracts more joy. Love attracts more love. And so on and so on. No one wants to attend a pity party, but everyone wants to attend a celebration. What do you want to attract? Put it out there and get ready to receive the returns.

Now furnish your spirit with things that are true: God's promises. He will provide. He will heal. He will restore. He will wipe away your tears. Joy will come in the morning, though weeping may endure for a night (Psalm 30:5). With His help you won't simply be a survivor. You will be an overcomer! Therefore, build your house. Build it on the Solid Rock.

And then move in.

➤ LOOKING INWARD ◄

- What is the state of your spiritual house?
- What do you believe about God? What are your areas of conflict between what you've been told and how you really feel about Him?
- Do you believe that you are important to God?
- What boundaries do you need to set in order to secure your peace?
- What promises from God's Word give you hope at this time?

➤ LOOKING UPWARD ◄

"I will show you what he is like who comes to me and hears my words and puts them into practice. He is like a man building a house, who dug down deep and laid the foundation on rock. When a flood came, the torrent struck that house but could not shake it, because it was well built. But the one who hears my words and does not put them into practice is like a man who built a house on the ground without a foundation. The moment the torrent struck that house, it collapsed and its destruction was complete" (Luke 6:47-49).

5

RUN FOR COVER

A pot filled with good things sits simmering on the stove. The room smells of its savory contents, though they are hidden under the lid. It is crucial to contain the steam inside the pot, infusing flavor and tenderizing the meat and vegetables. Only then can you get just the right consistency and bouquet. Sometimes we, too, need to go undercover for a season. To hide out in that house of truth we have built. Hide in the shelter of God's arms and silently ponder all He has revealed to us. Soak in it. Let it simmer. Get all the flavor and nutrients out of it. Allow it to preserve us, to get in our veins until our understanding of God's truth becomes a natural part of us.

After the angel of the Lord brought Elijah food and drink, the prophet went up to the mountain of God, entered a cave, and spent the night. In the darkness of his life, Elijah hid himself under the arm of his Savior and allowed One greater than himself to be his solace. It is true, "He who dwells in the shelter of the Most High will rest in the shadow of the Almighty" (Psalm 91:1). I can't think of a safer place.

Of course the divine King of all the universe will not allow us to hide from our problems indefinitely. When we come into His presence, we can expect Him to eventually confront us with probing questions. Perhaps that's why, although He offers us comfort and safety, we avoid being alone with Him. We are afraid of what He will tell us. But there comes a day when we have nowhere else to go *but* to Him. And when we do, these deep questions He asks will cause us to see ourselves as He sees us, and to discover the answers that have been there all along.

"What are you doing here?" God asked Elijah the inevitable question. Now, do you think God didn't know why Elijah was there? Of course He did. But He wanted Elijah to hear his own thinking. Have you ever been talking to someone who said something absolutely ridiculous? You might interrupt with "What did you just say?" Not because you didn't hear, but because you want that person to pay attention to the absurdity of the remark.

God knew that Elijah was feeling sorry for himself. Cut off from any help. Considering himself a lone, undeserving victim. After all, he had only done what God had called him to do. Now look at the mess he was in! Elijah answered, "I have been very zealous for the LORD God Almighty. The Israelites have rejected your covenant, broken down your altars, and put your prophets to death with the sword. I am the only one left, and now they are trying to kill me too" (1 Kings 19:10). *When are You going to show up, God? Isn't there any justice left in this world? I'm the only one trying to do the right thing, and where has it gotten me? How could You leave me hanging like this?*

We've all said it at one time or another. *I was the best wife I could be. How could he decide not to love me after all I tried to be for him? I did a good job; I went above and beyond the call of duty at work. How could they just phase out my position like that and replace me with someone younger?* Whatever your situation, the sense of overwhelming isolation is the same: *I'm the only one going through this. Hello? God, where are You?!*

When we ask questions of God, we must be prepared for His reply. God told Elijah to come out of the cave, stop hiding from his circumstances, and stand on the mountain in His presence. God will baby us only so long. In effect He says, *I want you to face Me, I want to reveal something about you and something about Myself to you. The limits you placed on yourself, as well as on Me, have brought you to this place. I want you to rise to a new level, a level beyond your current comfort. I am not going to come down to where you are.* God's Son Jesus did that for us. When we were bowed low in our sins, unable to rise in our own strength, He stripped Himself of all His heavenly trappings and descended to our level to pave the way for us to ascend with Him. He gave us an entry into heavenly places. God the Father expects us to use the pass that we were given in order to see Him.

Every time we ask Him why we are where we are, He will take that as an invitation to challenge us on where we stand. It is His desire for us to soar like an eagle above the storms of life, not crawl and cower beneath them. Unfortunately, sometimes only unbearable pressure makes us budge from our comfort zone. But if that's what it takes, then surely He will allow it. Our discomfort becomes His tool to bring us to a greater place.

So now that you are willing to get honest, take your cue. Go undercover for a while, but while you are there, examine yourself. If you don't like where you are, get out of your cave and get ready to rise.

➤ LOOKING INWARD ◆

- How long have you been in your cave? What line of thinking has made you feel helpless?
- What do you long to see happen during this time of hiding?
- What do you think God should do to fix your situation?
- What would help you gain a new perspective on your situation?
- Have you heard anything yet? What has God asked you to do to rise above your circumstances?
- What can you do to partner with God to get results?

➤ LOOKING UPWARD ◆

"He who dwells in the shelter of the Most High will rest in the shadow of the Almighty. I will say of the LORD, 'He is my refuge and my fortress, my God, in whom I trust.'... He will cover you with his feathers, and under his wings you will find refuge; his faithfulness will be your shield and rampart" (Psalm 91:1-2,4).

6

CLIMB HIGHER

When a plane encounters a storm, it doesn't try to land immediately. It seeks a higher altitude. It searches for a safe place above the storm where it can continue the journey. The winds and storms of life should signal us to do the same, yet we are more likely to either attempt an emergency landing or bail out completely. Or we frantically cast off anything we suspect as being part of our difficulty, throwing out the problems as well as the things that have no part of our problem. Whenever we're in panic mode, in the thick of things, we have no discernment. We make decisions based on impulse rather than careful consideration, and when the smoke clears, we find ourselves under a pile of bad decisions.

Pressure should cause us to rise, not fall. Fact: Storms will come. Expect them. Don't get thrown off course by the inevitable. Expect not to be liked. Rise above the rejection. Anticipate the weaknesses of other people to cause you problems. Rise above their manipulations. Count on things not always going your way. Rise above the opposition. Know that trouble will show up uninvited. That doesn't mean it has to stay and be your best friend. Rise above it. Go up higher where the air is too thin for the germs of fear and hopelessness to live and multiply.

After resting, eating, and drinking, our weary prophet Elijah traveled for forty days to get to the mountain of God. It might take a while to climb to higher ground, but you will get there if you set your sights on it. While others take the low road, choose a different path. Look up and see your help coming from above. Climb above all that distracts you from quieting your soul. Like produce in a Mason jar, we absorb the juices of what we soak in. Therefore seek silence. Seek fresh air. Seek God.

Elijah knew that only one person had anything of lasting import to say about his situation. He also knew that he couldn't hear the voice from where he was. He needed to get a bird's-eye view of his circumstances before he could make any more decisions about his course. Higher ground would put his fears beneath him, clear his thinking. And so he went in search of a better perspective. It took him a while, but he kept going and eventually got there.

How do we get to higher ground? By making the decision to pull ourselves up by our bootstraps and climbing. Ugh! You mean I have to do work?! Oh yes indeed! Snapping out of depression takes work. Decisions have to be made. You've got to get up. God did not get upset at Elijah for being depressed; however, He would not allow the prophet to remain that way indefinitely. He had to get up and move on. That's what the food and drink were all about—to equip Elijah for the journey.

The climb to higher ground is a spiritual one, though some physical work may also be required. Climbing in the spirit has to do with renewing your mind, maturing your thought life, your attitude, and what you believe God is able to do with the broken pieces you hold in your hand. He will never do what you expect. "As the heavens are higher than the earth," God says, "so are my ways higher than your ways and my thoughts than your thoughts" (Isaiah 55:9). Life looks quite different from where God sits. In order to get a clue, we need to see things from His point of view. This requires higher spiritual learning and a change in our perspective. This will not happen when we lie down on the job and allow ourselves to become paralyzed. Let your panic subside and become open to God's helpful instruction from His Word as well as from others who offer sound advice. Then get up. You have work to do. One step at a time. One foot in front of the other. Up, up, up. Until you reach a clear vantage point. The view will only change when you choose to climb.

➤ LOOKING INWARD ◄

- How long have you been in the same place?
- What will it take to propel you to the next level?

- What type of help do you expect from God and others? Will you get it where you are?
- What aspects of your thinking need to change?
- What can you do to change your thinking process? What decisions do you need to make?

➤ LOOKING UPWARD ◄

"The Sovereign LORD is my strength; he makes my feet like the feet of a deer, he enables me to go on the heights" (Habakkuk 3:19).

7

GET IN THE SPIRIT

Time has a way of getting us to see things God's way. This is why, if you want to rise to new levels, it is crucial to stay in contact with the only One who knows your tomorrows. Getting in the Spirit is not the same as remembering your spirit, as a popular talk-show host likes to advise. It is much bigger than that. Your own inner voice does not have enough information if it is not connected to the One who gave it breath. The One who created everything and everyone knows how everything is supposed to work. This is the One you want to know and hear from. You must get in *the* Spirit and stay there in order to hear what He is saying.

The Spirit of God is ready and willing to give us specific instructions on how to get from point A to point B. We have been promised a Comforter, a Teacher, and a Revealer of deep mysteries in the person of the Holy Spirit. Yet this is the Spirit that we either forget, take for granted, or refuse to acknowledge. We are far too busy trying to untangle the yarn of our lives by ourselves, only to find ourselves bound up in bigger knots. Yet the Holy Spirit offers a quiet invitation:

O people of Zion, who live in Jerusalem, you will weep no more. How gracious he will be when you cry for help! As soon as he hears, he will answer you. Although the Lord gives you the bread of adversity and the water of affliction, your teachers will be hidden no more; with your own eyes you will see them. Whether you turn to the right or to the left, your ears will hear a voice behind you, saying, "This is the way; walk in it." (Isaiah 30:19-21)

What a relief! You mean I don't have to figure it all out on my own? Absolutely not! "If any of you lacks wisdom, he should ask God, who gives generously to all without finding fault, and it will be given to him"(James 1:5). You cannot miss your appointment with destiny if you stay plugged into the source of power and wisdom. It is easy to be angry at God and cut Him off when we hurt or struggle. *After all,* we think, *He allowed this. He could have spared me all this pain with just a wave of His sovereign hand.* Ah, but we don't see the big picture. Though Elijah had a prophetic gift, even he could not know all the details of his situation. Despite his feelings he had to draw strength from the Spirit of God.

Let's take a look at Joseph, a young Israelite who dreamed twice of being a great leader before his jealous brothers sold him into slavery. Undaunted, and diligent even in slavery, Joseph gradually advanced to the head position in his master's house before being falsely accused of a crime and thrown into jail. Could his situation have been any worse?

So here is Joseph, minding his own business in jail when he runs into two of the king's employees. These men have had dreams, and they are looking for interpretations. Without hesitation Joseph interprets their dreams, and events come to pass just as he states they will!

(I have to make a note here. Remember that Joseph's whole story starts off with a dream. Whenever you see a recurring theme in Scripture or in life, you can be sure it is a key to unlocking the door of your destiny. What are the recurring themes in your life? Look at them closely; you may learn important things.)

How could Joseph know what was going to happen to these two men? In spite of his difficulties, Joseph didn't cut off God. Instead, he remained in close relationship with Him. And God revealed it to him, that's how. What God didn't reveal was how these men would be instrumental in getting Joseph out of jail and advancing him toward the leadership role he'd dreamed of. Stick with me now. When you don't know how to get out of your situation, trust God to do some networking for you. He is the One who orders our steps, encounters, and conversations. You never know who you are talking to. I have met people whom I wouldn't have glanced at had not something arrested my soul and caused me to stop and talk to them. Those same people sometimes turn out to be a blessing.

Once, after a two-day delay in London on my way to West Africa, I met two schoolgirls in the line at the airline counter. As we were subjected to yet another twelve-hour delay, I "adopted" these two young ladies after their escort had to leave them. When we finally landed in Ghana, we were greeted by quite an entourage! Their mother was the Minister of Tourism, and she extended VIP courtesies to me because I had safely escorted her children home. She rectified my situation with the airline and then on top of it all extended an amazing business opportunity to me as well. So you never know! An act of kindness can reap incredible blessings.

If we are too busy being buried in our circumstances to be sensitive to the promptings of the Spirit within, we will miss even more important providential moments. The world at large calls these "chance" meetings serendipitous, but in actuality they are God-ordained appointments. We can never know the capacity of others based on their appearance alone, nor can we foresee how being a blessing to them might turn out to be a blessing for us. Therefore it is wise to take no meeting for granted and to treat every person we meet with respect and an attitude of service. God's instruction on this is clear: "Do not forget to entertain strangers, for by so doing some people have entertained angels without knowing it" (Hebrews 13:2). This doesn't mean you have to take strangers into your home. Use wisdom. But don't regard anyone as unworthy of your attention either. Stop. Take the time to talk and listen. Consider their words. Seek to bless them. There might be a blessing in it for you—at the very least, the rewards of obedience.

Joseph couldn't see how going to jail factored into his dream of being a mighty leader one day, but God was actually keeping him on track for just that appointment. Who can solve the mystery of the way we each take? We simply do not have enough information from where we sit. God knows that. He doesn't always explain what He is doing, but that doesn't mean that He is not working on your behalf. We just get bent out of shape because we don't know what's going on.

> "For my thoughts are not your thoughts,
>> neither are your ways my ways," declares the LORD.
> "As the heavens are higher than the earth,
>> so are my ways higher than your ways
>> and my thoughts than your thoughts.
> As the rain and the snow
>> come down from heaven
> and do not return to it
>> without watering the earth
> and making it bud and flourish,
>> so that it yields seed for the sower and bread for the eater,
> so is my word that goes out from my mouth:
>> It will not return to me empty,
> but will accomplish what I desire
>> and achieve the purpose for which I sent it." (Isaiah 55:8-11)

But when God *does* decide to share what He is doing, we need to be listening. We need to be able to recognize His voice and move on what He says. The beauty of being in a place you cannot control is that it gives God the opportunity to work out His plan. You can plan your work all you want to, but in the end God will work His plan with or without your help. In the end, you will land on the spot where He has painted the X. If you don't partner with Him, it simply takes longer.

Joseph partnered with God even while he was in jail. The chief jailer put him in charge of all the prisoners, and Joseph had interpretations for those men's dreams that day because he had stayed connected to the Spirit of God. That was just the beginning of his breakthrough. If we want to move past where we are, like Joseph, we must strive to stay in the Spirit.

➤ LOOKING INWARD ◄

- What are you trying to figure out about your life right now?
- Who and what are your sources of counsel? Is their wisdom effective and in alignment with Scripture, or does it lead you to drink from sources that eventually run dry?
- How is your dialogue with God these days? Are you staying connected?
- Are you taking the time to listen to what God is saying?
- Can you let go of your opinions? Are you open to God's direction?

➤ LOOKING UPWARD ◄

"Since we live by the Spirit, let us keep in step with the Spirit" (Galatians 5:25).

WHEN LIFE ASSAULTS
YOUR FAITH

♛

He lived a good life. No. Correction. An incredible life. He was wealthy. Filthy rich. His businesses were prospering in unusual abundance. His future was secure. He had standing, not only in the community, but throughout the land. He had the respect of leaders and commoners alike. Others sought his wisdom, counsel, and charity. He gave freely and generously. His family life was sound. Good wife. Good children. They were a tight-knit, supportive clan. His employees were loyal. His reputation was flawless. He was a man of integrity. Blameless and God-fearing. Life was good. Real good. As a matter of fact, life was perfect.

But things changed. Suddenly. In a flash he became the victim of a hostile takeover that wiped out half his empire. Before he could catch his breath, terrorists bombed his business center and killed all his employees. His remaining holdings and work force were wiped out by the aggressive measures of those who took advantage of his precarious position. His stocks plummeted. All remaining money that he had on paper went up in smoke.

As if financial ruin was not enough, the news came shortly later that his children, who had been on a family outing, were on their way home in the family's private jet when a storm cut off their visibility. As they attempted to land, the violent winds caused them to crash. The plane exploded, killing them all instantly. All ten children, wiped out of his life forever, just like that.

The devastation wreaked havoc on his health. He aged twenty years in a day. He broke out in hives, which became infected. The doctors could not identify a cure and had no idea what to prescribe.

Suddenly his wonderful wife was not so understanding. Lost in her own grief, she found his inability to rise to the occasion repulsive. She offered no warmth or solace and rebuked even his request for physical comfort. Her honeyed tongue turned to acid. She spewed her own bitterness in the only advice she could bring herself to offer. "Just curse God and die!" His friends and associates fled as if his bad luck were contagious, and he was left alone to try to make sense of all that had befallen him.

Of course the man I am speaking of in modern terms, as I retell his story in Michelle paraphrase, is Job. But he could be you or me. Poor Job. An innocent victim. Some feel he was merely an unfortunate pawn of two greater powers in a bet. The story goes that Satan told God the only reason Job was such a good boy was because God had protected him from life's traumas. But God was so sure of the goodness of Job's heart He allowed Satan to test him; He would prove His slithery foe wrong. Though Job had his moments, he passed the test with flying colors.

How did Job maintain his sanity in the midst of such all-consuming chaos? What do you do when you've lost everything you've worked so hard to build over the years in one fatal swoop? When you've lost a loved one? How do you handle the heartache of a spouse kicking you when you're down? Rejecting you in the midst of your pain? Calling you a worthless failure? How do you deal with friends who turn their backs on you or, worse yet, show up to criticize you and implicate you as the cause of your own suffering? How do you find the path to restoration? How do you keep hope alive after facing the apparent evidence that even God has turned His back on you? How do you find your way back home to a life of peace, plenty, and prosperity? First you have to breathe. Again. And again. It will take conscious breathing for a certain amount of time before you can get your second wind.

PART II

GETTING YOUR SECOND WIND

Myth
Life owes you something.

➤ ➤ ➤

Truth
But godliness with contentment is great gain. For we brought nothing into the world, and we can take nothing out of it.

1 TIMOTHY 6:6-7

8

GET REAL

Let me take you back to Babylon where the Israelites got stuck for a moment. Do you know what God told the Israelites when their captors deposited them in enemy territory, even before visions of their homeland were a distant memory? In essence: "Build homes. Plant crops. Settle down. Marry. Have children. Because you won't be going anywhere for a while."

It does seem heartless of God to tell the Israelites so bluntly that they should just settle into bondage without complaint. Yet it wasn't out of cruelty that He gave them this information. He was just dealing with the facts. The facts, whether you like them or not, are still the facts. In order to change the facts, one must see them as they are. You've got to know what you're working with.

The fact is, your mate is not going to change overnight into the companion you've always dreamed of. The fact is, you will probably have to stay at that awful job and put up with that abusive boss a little longer. The fact is, that pile of debt will not disappear in the blink of an eye. The fact is, the heartache you feel over the death of your loved one will probably never entirely fade. Of course, there is always room for a miracle. But God picks the when and the where for those very carefully. The fact is, generally speaking, nothing in any of our lives is an instant fix. In some cases, fixes simply won't happen at all this side of heaven. Let's face it, your situation is going to take time to rectify.

Reality doesn't deny its predicament or believe that ignoring the dilemma will make it go away. Reality looks at the problem that seems larger than life and says, "Well, this is not the greatest situation, but there's no getting around it. So I will just deal with it little by little on a consistent basis until the problem is solved. That's the best I can do." Reality does what it can and leaves the rest to God. Between the two, the job gets done.

God was realistic when it came to the human race. While we often say that love is blind, I beg to differ. True love is realistic. Love sees things as they really are and comes up with a solution. God saw a world that needed a Savior, and He provided one. He didn't go into denial about the things we did that offended Him. Neither was He overwhelmed by our failings. He knew the debt we owed, knew we'd never be able to cover it, and He promptly paid it. The end. By God. He now leaves it up to us to decide if we want to cash the check He wrote for us.

However, that check doesn't enable us to escape the trials of life that groom us to be better citizens of His creation. "We also rejoice in our sufferings, because we know that suffering produces perseverance; perseverance, character; and character, hope. And hope does not disappoint us, because God has poured out his love into our hearts by the Holy Spirit, whom he has given us" (Romans 5:3-5). Well, this does give you another way to look at suffering, doesn't it? You can actually get something out of it. In the end, your suffering becomes a stage on which God can perform. And once you've viewed the performance, you will never again doubt His ability to delight you. Even when the plot stinks, you will rest assured of a happy ending.

In the meantime, though, you must learn to balance realistic thinking with spiritual hope. This means that you admit where you are and partner with God in taking practical steps toward your breakthrough. The solution to your problem just might be a lot simpler than you imagined. The thing required of you could almost be overlooked.

Jesus, when seated on a hill expounding about the kingdom of God to thousands, did not lose sight of the fact that though the crowd had been feeding on His words, they also needed to eat natural food. The reality: No one had anticipated the crowd, and the disciples had nothing to offer them. The solution: two fish and five loaves of bread. The disciples resigned themselves to going without. But Jesus had another perspective—from the vantage point of faith. He decided to work with what He had. He blessed the food and broke it. And broke it. And broke it. The end result? Everyone was fed, and there were even leftovers (Matthew 14:13-21)!

Sometimes being realistic means using your available resources. When God sent Moses to lead the people out of Israel, Moses knew he was no match for Pharaoh and his armies. What would he use to defend himself? How would he prove he had the power of God behind him? "What is that in your hand?" God asked him. "Throw it on the ground" (Exodus 4:2-3). All Moses had was a simple rod, but when cast down it unleashed signs and wonders. God was indeed behind Moses and meant business when it came to freeing His people. What do you have in your hand that you can use to begin to make a difference? Something small? That's all right. Begin to use it. Begin to bite chunks out of that big elephant that looms before you. He can be eaten. One bite at a time.

What is the reality of your situation? Do you care to even admit it? Before plans can be drawn up for any new building, a surveyor must first examine the lay of the land. He must know every nook and cranny, what he needs to work around, what he can bulldoze away. Assess your situation. Come up with a flexible plan within the boundaries of your reality for moving forward and getting what you want. Don't allow the unexpected occurrences that life has dealt to stop you. Factor that potential surprise into the equation of where you go from here. God told the Israelites they'd have seventy years to work with. There's the reality. Now they could unpack their bags and be about the business of living to the best of their ability.

I'm the type of person who is fine as long as I know what I'm dealing with. This person is crazy? Okay, I know how to deal with him. I won't get that check this week? All right, with a little bit of reshuffling I can make what I have work until it comes through. That opportunity is a bust?

Hmm, what are my other options? There is a way for the willing to overcome the obstacles life sets before us.

Being realistic should not be interpreted as lacking faith in God. King David, of whom God said, "My love will never be taken away from him," was good for stating the facts: "This is happening and that is happening, *but*"—there was always a but—"God is able to bring me through this." How could he be so confident? Because he knew who was really in charge. Not life. God! "When times are good, be happy; but when times are bad, consider: God has made the one as well as the other" (Ecclesiastes 7:14).

No, denial is not the way to go. Denial is paralyzing. Stagnant. Dead. Be honest about where you are, and make a list of your possibilities. I wonder what got Adam in bigger trouble with God: refusing to admit where he was and what he had done, or eating the forbidden fruit? I suspect, the first. Instead of just telling God where he was and what he had done, he waited to be discovered and then blamed both Eve and God for his predicament. Forget blaming others and pretending the undesirable didn't happen. It did. Admit it and decide where to go from here. Ask God to show you the way out of your misery and disappointment. But He can only do that if you let Him in by telling Him where you are.

This is not the time for pride or shame, but for just pure honesty. I hurt. I failed. I missed it. I'm clueless… Whatever! Nothing is too ridiculous in God's eyes. Why? Because God is realistic. He knows that things happen. People get sick. Loved ones die. Mates cheat. Mates leave! People hurt you. Businesses fail. Valuables are lost. Desires perish. He will still ask you where you are. He will still tell you to stretch out your hand and tell Him what is in it. "Nothing," you say? Well, that's simple enough. That means you can use that same hand to reach out to someone for help. Eeeuw! We hate that. And yet, according to the reality of your situation, that is what it is going to take to get over this hump. No matter how embarrassing. So be it. For the sake of survival. For the sake of getting past where you are. Deal with it. First things first: In order to get help, you must get real.

➤ LOOKING INWARD ◄

- What are you not willing to admit about your life?
- What have you done to avoid honesty about this issue in the past?
- Whom have you chosen to blame for your predicament?
- What resources do you have at your disposal to help you move forward?
- Do you need help? Are you willing to ask for it?

➤ LOOKING UPWARD ◄

"Then you will know the truth, and the truth will set you free" (John 8:32).

9

Don't Just Lay There! Wrestle!

In times when we are robbed of our faith, we have to wrestle to hold on to what is true. The floods of life will threaten the very foundation of what we believe, even if we've built our house on solid truths. If God is good, certainly He would not have allowed these things to happen to us; if He is *not* good, then whom do we have to turn to? That's a good question, and it has no answer apart from convictions firmly supported by Scripture. The truth is, God *is* good; we just don't always know what He is doing. His purposes are sometimes concealed, but they will be revealed eventually if only we can hold on to God.

You will only be resolute in clinging to God and His promises if your belief system about Him is solid and remains intact. Job's three well-intentioned but woefully misguided friends did their best to dismantle Job's faith as to where he stood with God, but Job would not allow his friends to sway him. He did not lapse into self-doubt. He calmly told his doomsday trio, "I have understanding as well as you; I am not inferior to you" (Job 12:3, KJV). After all, hadn't he taught them a thing or two himself?

He knew God is no respecter of persons, thinking one is better than the other. He knew the human race is collectively imperfect and in need of God's grace; therefore, he was not about to believe he had been singled out as an example. He knew God is a just and reasonable God. He believed, as David did, that "the LORD saves his anointed; he answers him from his holy heaven with the saving power of his right hand" (Psalm 20:6) and that "the LORD secures justice for the poor and upholds the cause of the needy" (Psalm 140:12).

Job was convinced his situation could be rectified if his friends would just shut up long enough for him to have a real heart-to-heart with God. And he told them as much: "Now that I have prepared my case, I know I will be vindicated" (Job 13:18). Now, there's an idea! Job didn't just pray. He *prepared* his prayer. No mindless ramblings and emotional dissertation here. He reviewed his life to see if anything was amiss and found nothing. He decided to remind God of his innocence as well as God's own promises according to the scriptural Law. Job knew his spiritual rights! He was confident he could approach God with clean hands and get a fair hearing. "For the eyes of the Lord are on the righteous and his ears are attentive to their prayer" (1 Peter 3:12).

Truly, God invites us to reason with Him no matter what our state. He promises to cleanse us and address our situation. When the Gentile woman asked Jesus to heal her daughter, Jesus replied by saying He had come only for the Jews. But she didn't let that stop her. She won His admiration and a miracle healing for her daughter by humbly pleading her case. "Even the dogs under the table eat the children's crumbs" (see Mark 7:24-30). How could He turn away from such an appeal for mercy? He couldn't. She had exercised not only faith, but clarity of purpose.

When we wrestle with God, we are really wrestling with ourselves. The Spirit of God reaches down into our spirit to draw out the impurities that stand between us and the blessings He wants us to have. Our flesh, however, will fight to the death to remain the same. Only our determination to hold on to God can loosen the grip our tenacious old nature longs to maintain. Genesis 32:24 records the wrestling match between Jacob (Joseph's father) and the Angel of the Lord. Jacob wrestled the Angel all night and refused to let go until He blessed him. The blessing came in the form of a new name: Jacob, "the supplanter," was renamed Israel, "prince," indicating a transformation in Jacob's character. Character change equals destiny change; Israel was ready to walk into his full inheritance. He could now be trusted with the things God wanted to give him.

Job also knew his situation was not bigger than God. He understood that nothing and no one could prevent God's purposes from being ful-filled. No setback, no disappointment, no disaster in his life was big enough to get past God's desk without already being factored into the design of his ultimate destiny. Somehow, though Job had no idea how, God's awesome plan would come together. With this truth firmly entrenched in his heart, he turned his attention toward the only One who could do any-thing about his situation and simply said, "I know that you can do all things; no plan of yours can be thwarted" (Job 42:2).

And if all else failed, well, Job knew where he was going if he died. He declared his faith to the One who held his life in His hands: "I know you will bring me down to death, to the place appointed for all the living" (Job 30:23). So it is for those of us who know what we believe. We can bear witness to the words of Jesus: "I know where I came from and where I am going" (John 8:14).

God promises that you, like the seed the farmer plants, will not be crushed and bruised forever. He knows when you've had enough. Unfor-tunately, most of us seem to measure our tolerance levels with a different measuring stick than God uses. But He who knows all things knows about the reserve of strength within you. Perhaps you are about to discover it for yourself. The refining process taking place in your life might call for a deeper level of trust than you have ever had to tap into before. When you get to the end of yourself and know nothing more, wrestle with your doubts and then cling to the fact that, as long as God is God, all is not lost.

➤ LOOKING INWARD ◄

- What questions are you wrestling with right now?
- Which of God's truths do you have the most trouble believ-ing? Why?
- What aspects of God's truth resound with you?
- What can you do to build your faith?

- What do you need from God at this time to convince you of His goodness? Will it make a difference if He chooses to do something different?

"Let us hold unswervingly to the hope we profess, for he who promised is faithful" (Hebrews 10:23).

SEEK THE TRUE SOLUTION

Seek the solution? What do you think I've been doing all this time, Michelle? That is exactly what I've been trying to do, and I haven't come up with a thing! I feel your frustration, trust me. But let me ask you this: Exactly what have you been seeking? I said seek the *true* solution, not *a* solution. There is a difference. At least in God's mind. God told His displaced people—remember those workaholic Israelites?—(in Michelle paraphrase), "Hey, when you come and talk to Me, I will listen to you. When you seek Me with all of your heart, then you will find Me, and I'll turn your situation around" (see Jeremiah 29:12-13). I'm sure the Israelites stuck in Babylon were shocked by this suggestion. After all, what did the prophet Jeremiah think they had been doing even as the Babylonians carted them away? Of course they had been praying! How ridiculous!

Ah, but what had they been praying for? This is the big question. Were they seeking *God* or seeking relief from their trouble? Were their prayers a long litany of instructions telling God what He should do about their situation? Or were they truly seeking *Him* to hear what He wanted to tell them about their dilemma? Speaking of things that make you go, "Hmmm…"

How much time do you think we generally spend in prayer really cultivating a relationship with God versus submitting a list of requests to Him? *God, do this. God, do that. And by the way, could You also do this? Talk to You later. Bye.* The end. By most. God has got to be wondering, *What kind of relationship is this?* That is not how my greatest relationships go. They are mutually satisfying because both parties are interested in the feelings and thoughts of each other. I think on more occasions than I'd care to consider God feels greatly ignored and, even more, greatly used. How many people only pray in a time of crisis or need? How many of us say, "Hello, God," just for the sake of saying hello? How many of us care how God feels about anything? He is God, yet most of the time we treat Him as a servant who is badly taken for granted.

Yet God remains faithful, coming to our rescue time and time again, until He has finally had enough. Not enough for *His* sake, but enough for *our* sake. He knows if we go any further without being in intimate relationship with Him, we will really hurt ourselves. And so He allows things to fall apart in order to get our attention. To redirect our focus. To get us centered on what is truly important. To clean the slate and give us a fresh start.

The story of Jonah sitting in the belly of the big fish always amuses me. The text says on the third day, *then* Jonah lifted up his eyes and prayed. Now, come on! Do you really think Jonah waited in waterlogged silence for three days before he prayed? I don't think so! I think Jonah's prayer *changed* on the third day, and God said, "Now you're talking!" I think Jonah had *plenty* to say from the time he was thrown overboard and hit the water until the time he realized he was in a great dilemma—as in, stuck in the gut of a fish. Something on the order of "Get me out of here, God!"

Finally, after getting no response to any of his suggestions, he changed his tune. He confessed some things, such as the fact that he was running away from God. He repented of other things, such as getting distracted by his own thoughts on how life should go and what he should be doing. He let go of a whole bunch of his own ideas. He cleaned his slate with God and became extremely open to God's point of view. Jonah came to the conclusion that "those who cling to worthless idols forfeit the grace that could be theirs" (Jonah 2:8).

Wow! *That* is a *major* revelation. As long as I cling to the way I believe my life should go and place that ideal above being open to God's design for my life, I will never get to sample any of the other possibilities that loom in front of me. I'll be stuck by my own predeterminations. I'll miss out on what God wants to do in my life because I think I know better. And God, being the perfect gentleman, will not intrude on my plans (chalk that up to a little gift He gave us called free will). But just perhaps God has a better idea, one He will not force on me until I look up and ask, "What do You think, God? I kinda thought things should go *this* way, but what do You have to say on the subject?"

When the fish of life swallows us up, we find ourselves in a very dark and uncomfortable place. The situation stinks, and we feel suffocated by the enormity of our circumstances. We may find ourselves speechless in the midst of our suffering. So I submit to you a new approach: Seek God, not the solution to your problem. Don't try to figure it out. Get into His head. Crawl into His heart. And really, really listen. Don't talk. Just listen. He will tell you things, open your eyes to see what you have missed, broaden your perspective, and give you understanding. He will give you a workable solution. In some cases the solution might be a series of instructions to get you on the path to healing and fulfillment. Though the solution might take a while to completely manifest itself, you will be able to walk in peace through your situation because you will have clarity. You can see your way through. Stop trying to fix a broken life before you contact the Manufacturer. You will need instructions.

Perhaps that seems too simple to you. *But…shouldn't I be doing something? I can't just sit somewhere waiting for a voice I'm not sure I can even hear! I'm trying to pay my rent. I'm trying to fix my marriage. I'm trying to…I'm trying to…You know…* Yes, I do know, but how will you know what to do if you don't know what to do? We are right back where we started. Back to being clueless about how to solve the puzzle of our life. Contacting God is far more fruitful than wearing out all your closest friends and associates on the subject. Sometimes God speaks to us through the people in our lives, but in general, have you ever noticed how the advice of others never seems to quite hit the spot? That's because your spirit knows you need more information than they are capable of giving. Only one Person has the scoop on the missing pieces: God.

Go ahead. You can do it. Throw up your hands. Take them off the wheel. Give up your ideas of how your life is supposed to go, and allow God to steer you in a new direction. Seek Him. Not because you want a solution to your problem, but simply because you are interested in Him. Affection and interest go a long way with God. Or with any of us for that matter. However, when it comes to God, He promises a generous, personalized return on the investment of your love in Him. He says, "Because you love me, I will rescue you because you acknowledge my name (who I am). You will call Me and I will answer you. I will be with you in trouble. I will deliver you and honor you. I will satisfy you and show you my salvation" (see Psalm 91:14-16). Well! I think that includes everything you were looking for, wouldn't you say? So perhaps the way to get what we want from God is to give Him what He wants first, worshipers who seek Him. He is the true solution.

➤ LOOKING INWARD ⬻

- What is your prayer life like?
- When was the last time you spoke to God without a personal agenda?
- Where is your focus? What has been most important to you, survival or God's plan?
- Who and what are the idols—those things you think you can't do without—in your life?
- What preconceived notions stand between you and your breakthrough?

➤ LOOKING UPWARD ⬻

"Call to me and I will answer you and tell you great and unsearchable things you do not know" (Jeremiah 33:3).

GET HELP

What was God thinking when He told the captured Israelites to get married and have children in Babylon? As if building houses and planting gardens in a foreign land were not difficult enough! He was urging His people to increase rather than decrease. To not give in to the urge to shrivel up in a corner and die, but to stand up and make their presence known. To add to their allies. To work on their relationships. To become a force to be reckoned with. Even though they were feeling stuck.

Something happens when we can get over ourselves and reach out to others. Although God is our true solution, we should pay attention to the people He places in our lives, people who love us, love Him, and want to be of help. They partner with us and assist us in our journey. Truly there is strength in numbers.

The first temptation we have to resist when we are blindsided by trial is the urge to go into seclusion. Though a time away with God is good, we also must stay plugged in to those who can stand with us and believe with us for victory. Depression makes us run away from those who care about our situation. It becomes hard to lift and separate enemies from friends when we are drowning in disappointment and pain. Will that well-meaning friend utter words we are not ready to hear? Will words of encouragement be enough? Or leave us feeling worse? It's a chance you can't take. So you withdraw.

A man's business falls apart, and the demise of his marriage follows. Why? In the midst of overwhelming trial, he turns inward and repels the one person, his wife, who can gird him up. A woman's shame at yet another failed relationship causes the disintegration of an important friendship. Why? She fears the "I told you so…" of the one who lovingly tried to point out the warning signs along the way. Both the businessman and the brokenhearted woman need the friend who has been there through the good, the not so good, and the terrible. And yet they become so self-consumed with their present suffering that they don't see the arms waiting to hold and comfort them. They never turn a listening ear to receive the counsel that could heal them and help them begin again.

Some of us take ourselves way too seriously, making it impossible for others to help us. We are not open to advice. We shut ourselves off from any option or person who could give us aid. Shame convinces us to die in secret.

But God encourages us to reach out to others when we find ourselves in an undesirable situation. When Elijah's assistant betrayed him, God told him to get a new one. What if Elijah had said, "Oh no, God. I don't want a new assistant. The last one I had went behind my back and did things I told him not to do. I'll never trust another assistant again!" He would have missed out on God's plan. Instead, he took on Elisha and found himself strengthened enough to establish an entire school of prophets, to train others to continue his work. Elijah needed Elisha in his life to keep him from relaxing. To keep him from giving up. To keep him from holding back, protecting himself, and no longer doing his best work. This was not a luxury Elijah could afford if he was to fulfill God's purpose of raising up someone to complete the work he had started.

It is called accountability. People with no accountability run amuck, drunk on their own power or burned out by being exposed to far too much that makes them cynical and jaded. We all need someone in our life who helps keep us on course. Gives us fresh inspiration. Detects subtle shifts in our attitude that warn of upcoming problems. Everyone needs someone to remain transparent with and accountable to. Someone who is not a yes-man, but who loves us enough to question our actions and motives. To encourage us to even greater feats. To strengthen us when we grow weary.

So God instructed the Israelites to marry. How could one think of marriage at a time like this? As a captive, you don't feel deserving of alliances or attention. You feel unqualified and undesirable. You feel as though you've got to get back on top of your game before anyone would want to be a part of your world. When you've lost everything and your tomorrow seems uncertain, the mind reasons this is the time to batten down the hatches, to turn all attention toward recovery—financial or otherwise—and self-preservation. Relationships will have to wait. People will just have to understand that you are losing it. And if they can't...well, perhaps you are better off without them. If they can't help by getting out of the way, then indeed they are a hindrance.

Not true, not true! Let's look at this issue of relationships from a broader perspective: covenant. Now, a covenant is different from a contract. A contract has conditions, terms, and time parameters. A covenant has none of those. A covenant is a promise of trust and love, a pledge to stand together no matter what, forever and ever amen. When God instructed the Israelites to marry, He was saying, "Make covenants with one another. Build a community. Spread out and occupy. Have children." Children are the natural extension, the fruit of the marriage covenant. Bear fruit—comfort, hope, encouragement, assistance—from the other covenants you make. Fruit that takes you from merely living under the circumstances to rising above them and leaping over your present situation. Fruit is the forerunner of increase.

Covenant relationships, resulting in the community of faith, keep us alive in crucial times. For better, for worse, for richer, for poorer, in sickness and in health—these vows should not be confined to the covenant of marriage. They should be true of friendships as well. Covenant is not always a cushy, comfortable place. The bottom line of covenant is *I am going to do what's best for you whether you like it or not.* Sometimes our loved ones will have to say and do things that are not pretty while we are feeling sorry for ourselves, but in the end their actions safeguard our very life. Even if the truth of the wisdom stings, so be it. Taking medicine has never been delightful, but after the bitter taste comes healing. Family and

friends, siblings and mates are the hands of God. Iron sharpening iron.
Pruning. Clearing away the rubbish. The things that hinder your growth.
Those in covenant relationship with you will not let you die. They are
determined to harvest fruit from the lives of their loved ones at all costs.
Allow them to till the soil of your life when you can't. There is no shame in
this. There will be another season when it will be your turn to do the same
for them.

King Solomon, David's son and old man wisdom himself, came to the
conclusion that

> Two are better than one,
>> because they have a good return for their work:
> If one falls down,
>> his friend can help him up.
> But pity the man who falls
>> and has no one to help him up!
> Also, if two lie down together, they will keep warm.
>> But how can one keep warm alone?
> Though one may be overpowered,
>> two can defend themselves.
>> A cord of three strands is not quickly broken.
>> (Ecclesiastes 4:9-12)

Life is cold when you try to live it alone. You need covenant relationships,
a community of support, with God as the ever-present glue at the center
to help you hold life together.

Even geese know this. Yes, I'm talking about those winged creatures
that go "honk!" They all fly in the same direction, in formation, because
they are carried on the current of the wind they create corporately with
their wings. This "jet stream" buoys them up and gives them their height.
The leaders of the formation take turns at the key point of the V position—where there is no air current to ride—in order to keep any one of
the group from becoming exhausted. If a goose gets out of line, two geese

are dispatched to lead it back on track. If it continues to drift out of the formation, all the geese surround their fellow feathered friend by placing it in the middle to gently ensure it stays on course. If a goose falls or is shot down, two geese go to its rescue. If it is wounded, they will not leave the goose to die alone. That goose will die with two geese in attendance. Geese believe in community. Their natural instincts are to bind together in an unbreakable covenant no matter what. Sometimes I think animals are smarter than people. We could take a lesson from our feathered friends, a very simple lesson: We all need one another.

We were not created to be independent agents. We were made with a dependency for intimacy with God and fellowship with mankind. When one of these areas suffers, we cling to something less conducive to our good in order to fill the void. Other props and addictions take their place. Not to our benefit but to our destruction. When we refuse to admit we need help, we become helpless and miserable people.

If I decide to diet on my own, I can fall off the horse at any given moment. But if I'm attending Weight Watchers and I know I have to face someone standing over a scale, I toe the line. I can't endure the shame of failure in front of my counselor. Accountability is the silent guardian that makes you do the right thing even when you don't feel inclined to do so.

The observance has been made that "for lack of guidance a nation falls, but many advisers make victory sure" (Proverbs 11:14). Accountability provides you with sound counsel and keeps you on track. Transparency keeps you faithful. And covenant with others helps you handle what you cannot fix.

So allow yourself to be surrounded by the caring counsel of others. Let them hold up your arms when you no longer can exercise your faith to hold on. Do not isolate yourself. In that lonely place lurks a dangerous enemy called deception who will lure you to a remote place and finish you off with a final thrust of despair. Cling to family. Build rather than tear down. Draw closer instead of withdrawing. Bind yourself to your friends. Embrace rather than repel. Reach out; do not become self-absorbed.

Whatever your situation, you need someone. Family and friends are not the enemy. You are not alone. They understand more than you know. Shame will not help you. Your loved ones will. So continue to enlarge your community, honor your covenants, and harvest the fruit they help you bear.

➤ LOOKING INWARD ◄

- Have you reached out to someone or withdrawn in your pain and disappointment? Why?
- Is there someone you trust to share your concerns with? Are you willing to involve that person?
- What keeps you from being transparent with those who can help?
- What would be of help to you at this time? What are you willing to do to get it?
- What steps will you take to reach out in your situation rather than withdrawing?

➤ LOOKING UPWARD ◄

"For waging war you need guidance, and for victory many advisers" (Proverbs 24:6).

DISCARD
NEGATIVE ADVICE

Perhaps one of the more difficult aspects of reaching out for help is sorting through the relative wisdom of those who are in covenant with you. "Curse God and die," Job's wife told him. Whoa! Maybe Job's wife thought God didn't have any thunderbolts left. It is not wise to curse the only One who can help you. But in her mind—operating out of present suffering—God's former goodness and the record of all the delights she had enjoyed at His hands were quickly forgotten. This was not a woman who would search herself to see whether she was responsible for any of their misfortunes before laying the blame elsewhere. In her mind, none of their suffering was Job's fault. Or her fault. They were victims of circumstance. Victims of other peoples' unchecked greed and of evil. Victims of the forces of nature. If God is so powerful and so loving, why didn't He prevent all this? We'll get to that question, but for now let's go one step at a time.

Piling negative thoughts and words on top of already negative circumstances would not prove helpful. Even in the midst of his suffering, Job understood this and rebuked her. "He replied, 'You are talking like a foolish woman. Shall we accept good from God, and not trouble?' In all this, Job did not sin in what he said" (Job 2:10). Yes, we can sin with our mouths. We can stir up a lot of trouble with our mouths.

It is important for us to understand how much power we and others have in our spoken words. We are made in the image of God. The same

DISCARD NEGATIVE ADVICE 67

God who spoke everything into existence. We are not told that He waved a magic wand or did something magical. The Bible very simply and directly says that God *said,* "Let there be"—and there was! Just like that. Because we are made in His image, that means we also have His same creative power. Therefore, watch your words! "The tongue has the power of life and death, and those who love it will eat its fruit" (Proverbs 18:21). "The tongue also is a fire.... It corrupts the whole person, sets the whole course of his life on fire" (James 3:6).

Have you ever been angry about something, and the more you talked about it, the angrier you became? You were stirring up the embers of a fire that would have eventually died. You created more anger.

Have you ever noticed that speaking a negative expectation about something or someone set you up for the fatal end that you anticipated? An impulsive word spoken in haste can cause more damage in a single moment than we ever imagined. Whether our words are an automatic reaction to whatever it is we are going through or spoken in measured thoughtfulness, it doesn't matter. The end result is the same: disaster. We are left muttering those famous words, "I wish I hadn't said anything."

Consider David in the wilderness, fleeing for his life from King Saul. Not only is he on the run, but there are others depending on him. Men who have chosen to be loyal to him. The stress must have been overwhelming. Yet David chose not to speak or do anything against the madman who was after him. David was not in denial about what was going on, believe me, but he stayed focused on the solution rather than the problem. Better yet, he chose to *declare* the solution by speaking of God's ability to deliver him at the right time. In the end David was avenged and exalted. The struggle proved worthwhile.

Why bother rehearsing the negative? The negative already exists! Why not focus all your energy on changing for the better? The bottom line is this: Every day of our lives we have a choice. To choose life or death, blessings or curses. We may not have power over anything else that is going on around us. But we do have power over our lips and the words that we choose to say. So choose wisely.

Friends come. Well-meaning friends who will cause you to question where you are, just as Job's friends did. Are you at fault? Is God ignoring you? How could this happen if you are friends with God? Are you *sure* you didn't do something wrong? How is your prayer life? On and on the questions come in your friends' desperate attempt to get to the root of your suffering. Not meaning to be negative, they sometimes are. Don't go there with these people. Separate the hard but true words from the ungodly observations. If what a person says to you doesn't line up with the Word of God, toss it out. Remember, when people don't know what to say, they often say the wrong thing.

Small wonder the Shunammite woman, whose story appears in 2 Kings chapter 4, did not tell anyone about the death of her son. She simply uttered, "All shall be well," and went in search of the man who could do something about her situation. She knew her husband and her friends would have buried her son and called it a day. But she expected God to show up and turn things around. Her faith in the Almighty kept her going. Her faith restored what had been lost. Although we may not be able to expect our dead brought back to life, we can always expect God to breathe restoration into our life. Into our souls.

Are you facing more negative advice than positive reinforcement? Keep still. Wait to hear the word that can bring change. Find people who have triumphed in similar circumstances and seek their counsel. Cling to your faith in God, cling to His words, and discard negative advice.

➤ LOOKING INWARD ◄
- What have you been saying about your situation?
- What advice have you been receiving?
- How will you evaluate the wisdom of others' advice to you now and in the future?

- Do you think you have God's perspective on where you are?
  Why or why not?
- Can you trust God to bring something positive out of the
  negative?

➤ LOOKING UPWARD ◄

"We demolish arguments and every pretension that sets itself up against the knowledge of God, and we take captive every thought to make it obedient to Christ" (2 Corinthians 10:5).

DON'T ASK WHY, ASK WHAT

A popular commercial asks a profound question: "Why ask why?" Exactly! Do you ever get an answer that you are willing to accept when you ask this question in regard to your troubles? Though our friend Job was prone to reflecting on good days gone by, he never asked the question "Why me?" Perhaps he knew instinctively that the sovereign God of the universe didn't exactly owe him an explanation.

As a child I was raised with these words ringing in my ears: "Because I said so!" I can't say I ever received this reply to my questions very enthusiastically, but it *did* teach me to honor authority. As I grew older I learned that those "because-I-said-so" folks, namely my parents, actually knew what they were doing even if they didn't let me in on it. Eventually I learned to relax and trust their direction.

This is difficult. We all have ideas about how God should steer the ship of our life. When we don't like the direction things are going in, we are quick to say, "Wait a minute! Hold up! What's going on here?!" Job didn't go there. He merely stated (in Michelle paraphrase), "Oh well. God gives us everything, so why should we complain when He decides to take something back? He has the right to do as He pleases. And who could stop Him anyway?" (See Job 9:12.)

Now, I must add here that, based on some of the comments a hurting Job made, he had some pretty interesting but not altogether true ideas about God. They definitely put his wisdom in perspective. Though Job was considered one of the most knowledgeable men in the land, even *he* did not know *everything* about God. Some of his comments were purely speculation based on where he lived at present. To say that the Almighty had denied him justice and embittered his soul (Job 27:2)? C'mon, Job! In the midst of pain and turmoil, we are all prone to make statements about God that would make one raise an eyebrow of inquiry, "Oh really?!" No, *not* really, but our pain drives us to say things in hopes of jolting God out of His silence. To make Him say *something*, do *anything*, just give us a sign that He is actually present and wants to do something about our circumstances. So we hurl insults toward heaven: "God doesn't care about me! He *wants* me to be miserable!" Still, He remains strangely silent during these times, not moved by our jabs at Him, not in any hurry to prove Himself one way or the other.

Why would God allow such a thing to happen and then leave me to writhe in agony? That is not the question we should ask. In any case, having the answer wouldn't take away the pain. After Jonah, our deep-sea-diving friend, went to all the trouble to go to Nineveh and warn the citizens of impending doom if they didn't straighten up, they actually did. And God changed His mind about destroying the people who once lived according to evil. Jonah did not accept this turn of events graciously; Jonah pouted under the broom tree because he felt God had made him look like a false prophet and a complete idiot. God had to remind him that something bigger was going on than what Jonah simply thought his enemies deserved. Our situation, no matter what, is a small speck in the universal picture. It is one domino that, when tapped, sets off a ripple effect in the kingdom, spiritually as well as physically. One occurrence begets another occurrence.

What is God trying to do? Now, that's a better question. What is He trying to accomplish in my life? What is He trying to get out of me? What is He trying to put in? What area of my life is He trying to transform by renewing my mind in this instance? Is there a new way that I should look at death? loss? life? love? the pursuit of love? all that I hold dear? Has something subconsciously become an idol? What needs to be readjusted in my thinking? My way of life?

WHAT DOES GOD WANT FROM ME?! If there is a question to be asked, that is most certainly it. Not shouted in frustration, but said from the heart because you sincerely want to know and comply. Sometimes I think the fight we have with God in the aftermath of disturbing occurrences brings greater pain than the actual trial we experience. Fighting with God is not the same as wrestling with Him. Every time we shake our puny fist *at* Him rather than clinging to Him until we have an answer, we get in trouble.

Holding on to our perceived rights can be traumatic. It seems that the more we insist on our way and our rights, heaven digs in its heels in obstinate defiance against us, as if to prove who's really running things. But the minute we are able to say as Job did (in Michelle paraphrase), "God can do as He wishes; who am I to ask why He does what He does?" we are released to receive an answer, a new hope, the peace we're seeking, whatever! Though we can rest in the knowledge of a clean conscience before God, we must also yield to His sovereignty. As a matter of fact, knowing we are in right standing with Him should make doing so easier.

I recall missing a flight connection once because my original flight was an hour late. Upon arriving at the airport, I tried to secure a new reservation to finish my trip. The next flight I could be confirmed on was at 6 P.M. All other flights were booked solid. It was now 11 A.M. If I had to wait, could I upgrade to first class? I was exhausted and not looking forward to being squashed in a middle seat for five hours after waiting seven hours. No on that count too. Reconciling myself to the situation, I let go of my anger toward the airline for putting me in this situation in the first place and decided to try going standby on an earlier flight. If I was going to be sandwiched, I might as well be sandwiched earlier. I approached the desk and humbly asked the ticket agent, "Is there any possibility I could get on this flight standby? *I am willing to take any seat you have.* I just want to go home." After giving me a sympathetic smile, she handed me a ticket and waved me onward.

As I approached the plane, I realized it was one of those new double-decker planes. I was directed to proceed up the stairs to business class. Let me tell you, if this was merely business class, I have no idea what else they could have added to make first class any better! (It seems I learn most of my lessons these days while flying.) I wonder what the outcome would have been if I had approached the woman at the counter with an attitude. It's a small thing, but a worthy example of what happens if we free others—and God—of what we view as their obligations toward us.

What does God owe us? Absolutely nothing. He has already given us everything. His dearest and His best: His only begotten Son. Ah, but what do we owe God? Absolutely everything, and yet we give so little. Could it be in these painful times that God is calling us to self-examination, to consideration of what we have withheld from Him? The irony of it all is that we will never have enough to give, and in the end He asks for little. Our attention. Our worship. Our surrender of ourselves and all we cling to.

In truth, we cannot hold on to any of it, and yet we try vehemently to do so. So many times we stand guilty of compartmentalizing God. Telling Him what He does or does not have access to in our lives. Then, when disaster strikes in one of the areas that has been off limits to Him, we wonder where He is. I'll tell you where He is. He is standing close, weeping over your distress. My friend, the question is not "How can a God of love allow such things to happen?" The question is "What is He trying to get us to see and become?"

➤ LOOKING INWARD ➤

- Which areas of your life are off limits to God?
- Do you struggle with trusting God's agenda for your life? Why?
- What are the questions that plague you at this time?
- Where can you go for real answers?
- What are some things you can do to begin living as if you know God's divine plan is bigger than your own circumstances?

➤ LOOKING UPWARD ➤

"If any of you lacks wisdom, he should ask God, who gives generously to all without finding fault, and it will be given to him" (James 1:5).

LEAVE YOUR DEFENSE TO GOD

Faced with his friends' varying opinions as to why he was going through his trial, Job finally realized he had to leave his defense to God. Job had no explanation for his suffering, though he knew he had done nothing wrong. I'm sorry to break it to you, but being right doesn't always make you an automatic winner in this life. Although rightness will work in your favor in the end, it might cause more problems in the beginning.

Remember our friend Joseph, who was thrown in jail for a crime he didn't commit? Here's the story: Joseph's boss, Potiphar, had a wife who let her wandering eyes drift Joseph's way. Mrs. Potiphar repeatedly attempted to seduce him, and when she failed, she got downright ornery. Threw a fit, lied, accused him of rape! Her poor husband had to do something to keep the peace, though I doubt he believed his wife. This is where Joseph's integrity helped him. You see, a person who has integrity has it across the board. Joseph had handled Potiphar's money, and none had come up missing. He had access to everything in Potiphar's house, and there was no record of theft. Therefore it would have been hard for Potiphar to reconcile this new and outlandish accusation in the face of Joseph's consistently honest and upright behavior. So instead of having Joseph killed, which was the legal punishment for such an offense, Potiphar threw him into jail.

"Jail!" you say. "What type of consolation was that?" you wonder. The consolation came because, as the story goes, God was with Joseph in the jail. Not just *any* jail. The *king's* jail. I believe that sometimes while we're busy doing all the right things, God allows us to go to a place that *feels* like bondage. But it is *not* a punishment; it is a *safe place*. We're out of harm's way while God works on the bigger issues concerning our life. The great things to come. If He allowed us to remain in too comfortable a place, we wouldn't be willing to move on to the next level He has prepared for us. So He allows us to sit in a place where everything within us screams, "Get me out of here!"

Notice there is no record of Joseph even trying to defend himself against the wife's accusations. He simply went down to jail believing God would deal with everyone concerned. How could he be so confident? Because of his innocence. He had done nothing to warrant God's distraction from delivering him. When Joseph went to jail, God went to jail with him. He created favor for Joseph in the jail, and next thing you know, as I've mentioned already, Joseph was running the place!

Whether we are in a place of our choosing, whether we are in a place where we feel constricted or paralyzed, we can thrive. The only hindrance to rising to the top is us.

Someone told me once that I suffer graciously. I believe I have no choice. I am too determined to get to the blessing. I refuse to be distracted by the lies life tries to tell. As I lay in bed for a year and a half struggling to recuperate from a car accident, I did not allow my inability to walk to keep me from doing something with my hands. With my leg in a cast, propped in the air, I wrote my first book. It was something I had failed to do when I was freely mobile. I could only do what I could do; the rest of the issues I left to God. How was I going to live when I couldn't get around to work? I had to rely on God. When worker's compensation turned down my claim, I had to rely on God. And God came through with flying colors. Just a month before I had my accident, I had been asked to work for a client on retainer. They were to pay me a certain fee every month whether I worked or not. My part was to be available. No contract had been signed when my accident occurred. Yet God moved on my employer to honor his verbal agreement. All I can tell you is that there is no dark hole too large for God to light the way out.

As David said to God:

If I go up to the heavens, you are there;
 if I make my bed in the depths, you are there.
If I rise on the wings of the dawn,
 if I settle on the far side of the sea,
even there your hand will guide me,
 your right hand will hold me fast.
If I say, "Surely the darkness will hide me
 and the light become night around me,"
even the darkness will not be dark to you;
 the night will shine like the day,
 for darkness is as light to you.
 (Psalm 139:8-12)

Joseph rested in a similar knowledge and waited for God to reveal His hand. Stay clear on this one truth: Joseph didn't resign his dreams and longings. He merely tucked them deeper inside his heart and dealt with the present. In the present he needed a miracle. And God was setting him up for exactly that.

If you try to make things happen when you are in the king's prison, you will only deepen your frustration. Trust me, you won't be released a day earlier or later than scheduled by your Divine Keeper. Don't try to state your own defense; it will fall on deaf ears because God is more determined to get you where He wants to get you than to deal with your temporary relief. Jesus knew this, so in the face of His lying accusers, He stood silent, "led like a lamb to the slaughter" (Isaiah 53:7). He knew then what you need to know now in your situation: Those who seek your pain and your demise are only setting you up for greater blessings. Now, *that* is something to shout about. You know something that your enemies don't know. They are helping you get where you want to go. Of course it's not exactly the route you would have taken, but hey, whatever works.

You might not be in a position where someone is wrongly accusing you. Perhaps someone is denying you an opportunity you deserve. Perhaps someone is overlooking your goodness and rejecting you or betraying you. Maybe someone is holding something back from you that he or she could easily give. You fill in the blank. But when you do, release your desire to fight—and wait on God's timely defense.

➤ **LOOKING INWARD** ◄

- What area of injustice in your own life troubles you most right now?
- What defense have you been tempted to plead?
- Have your attempts worked at all? What have been the results?
- Have you factored God into the equation? How long are you willing to struggle before you do?
- How does your ability to right the wrong in your life compare to God's?

➤ **LOOKING UPWARD** ◄

"Even now my witness is in heaven; my advocate is on high" (Job 16:19).

UNDERSTAND THE SEASON

One of my favorite phrases in the Bible is "and it came to pass." Good times, bad times, they all come to pass. Nothing comes to stay indefinitely, although it may seem otherwise. The one constant in life is change. As the natural seasons change, so do the seasons of our lives. Some seasons are longer than others, but still they all eventually change. When *you* won't change, the winds of change will propel you forward—or backward—anyway. Count on it.

The only way you can ride the winds of change, as opposed to being swept away by them, is to understand the season you find yourself in. Understand its purpose and make the season work *for* you, not against you. Jesus understood and knew the seasons of His life. He told His disciples, "As long as it is day, we must do the work of him who sent me. Night is coming, when no one can work" (John 9:4). In other words, "Don't think we will be able to run around boldly proclaiming the good news indefinitely. There will come a time when people won't want to hear it. Your biggest fans today will be your greatest critics tomorrow. So stay focused and do as much as you can while you can. Face the fact that we are the flavor of the month for now, but people's tastes change."

The swinging pendulum of popularity is pretty obvious in today's culture. Stars rise and fall. The hot new look of the season today is passé tomorrow. So when you're not at the top of the A-list, don't take it personally. This is merely the cycle of life. What goes up must come down. Be willing to go down.

The world resists this idea of "going down." After all, the way up is to keep climbing, right? Not exactly. In God's kingdom the way up is down first.

Your attitude should be the same as that of Christ Jesus:

Who, being in very nature God,
>   did not consider equality with God something to be grasped,
> but made himself nothing,
>   taking the very nature of a servant,
>   being made in human likeness.
> And being found in appearance as a man,
>   he humbled himself
>   and became obedient to death—even death on a cross!
> Therefore God exalted him to the highest place
>   and gave him the name that is above every name,
> that at the name of Jesus every knee should bow,
>   in heaven and on earth and under the earth,
> and every tongue confess that Jesus Christ is Lord,
>   to the glory of God the Father. (Philippians 2:5-11)

For every descent into the valley, you can bank on an ascent to the mountaintop if you keep things in perspective and maintain your faith. I always wonder what went through Jesus' head as men mocked Him, spit on Him, and left Him to stumble under the weight of a cross. Did His thoughts turn to His former glory at that time? Did He want to cry out, "Do you know who you're messing with?"

Jesus did not think it beneath Him to become a servant. Servanthood is not a popular concept in today's society, yet the King of kings became a servant! Why? Because He understood that He had to give something in order to get what He desired. After all, anything worth having usually costs us something. Jesus humbled Himself and gave of Himself completely in obedience to God for the salvation of all mankind.

We, too, must be willing to pay a price for the fulfillment of our dreams. Who are we to think we can take shortcuts in the process of rising to the top? There is no room for feelings of entitlement on this journey of life. We must be willing to pass through the valley of humility in order to reach the high places. Our character is forged in this valley, the character we will need to keep all we have acquired—from profound revelation to a longed-for relationship to material wealth. God will only give us what He can trust us to handle correctly. And so He waits until sound character is forged in us.

Before young David became the king of Israel, he served the reigning king. Just think: There he is, out in the pasture minding his own business, with no great aspirations that we know of, settled into a life of tending sheep. All of a sudden he is beckoned to his father's house and anointed by a prominent prophet, who tells him he is going to be the king of Israel. Kind of hard to go back to tending sheep after being told something like that, isn't it? But David neither became arrogant in his expectations nor tried to make them happen. He hid the prophet's words in his heart and waited for the time to come. In the meantime, the task of daily living beckoned him.

Shortly after his anointing, David was summoned to the palace to play the harp and sing for King Saul's pleasure. That must have been an encouraging sign. But life at the palace was not what he expected. The king had fits and attempted to kill him even while David was serving him! But did David scratch his head and wonder if the prophet had been wrong? Did he put his hand on his hip and say, "Now, is that any way to treat the future king of Israel?" No, he did not. He escaped the attempt on his life and remained humble and forgiving toward his temperamental employer. He stayed focused on his job and clung to God.

God protected David in such an obvious way that ol' King Saul had to change his tactics. He decided to send David off to war, hoping he would be killed on the front line. You better believe that before you cash in on a big blessing, the enemy of your soul will try to take you out first. But the Lord was with David and made him successful in battle, just as he will make you successful in your trial if you don't give up or faint.

Well, what's a frustrated king to do when he's feeling threatened by an up-and-coming star whom all the people love? Become more intense about putting the source of the threat in the line of fire, of course. So Saul offered David one of his daughters to wed on the condition that he fight in a dangerous crusade. Then he sat back and banked on David's demise. But cream will always rise to the top no matter how far you push it down. God gave David success after King Saul's every attempt to do him in.

Now why would God allow David to go through such hard times if He loved him so much, if David was truly the one He had chosen for such a high and hallowed position? Because the title doesn't make the man. What's inside does. All pride and grandiose ideals had to be purged out of David. And so it goes with us. If you are harboring a big dream, get ready to endure the process of purification before attaining your desire. King Saul didn't go through anything before becoming king, and he turned out to be a foolish, prideful leader who was self-centered, not God-centered. His lack of character and his foolish decisions cost him his throne. David was not perfect, but the thing that distinguished him from the former monarch and made him a great leader was simple: He always remained open to God's touch and correction.

Though David had not anticipated the events on the pathway to the throne, he maintained his faith in God. As he wandered in the wilderness, running for his life from Saul year after year, he believed that if the prophet's words were truly from God, they would come to pass at the appropriate time. No one could stop his kingship from happening if it was really part of a divine plan. He understood, "There is a time for everything, and a season for every activity under heaven…[God] has made everything beautiful in its time. He has also set eternity in the hearts of men; yet they cannot fathom what God has done from beginning to end" (Ecclesiastes 3:1,11).

This was a lesson David was able to teach to his son Solomon, who later inherited his throne. Solomon authored the words of Ecclesiastes, though I'm sure they were loaded with his father David's influence:

> I know that there is nothing better for men than to be happy and
> do good while they live. That everyone may eat and drink, and find

satisfaction in all his toil—this is the gift of God. I know that
everything God does will endure forever; nothing can be added to it
and nothing taken from it. God does it so that men will revere him.
(Ecclesiastes 3:12-14)

While many gaze with envy on the successes of others (marital, financial, career), the story of what it took to get where they are is often overlooked. What trials. What disappointments. What unexpected twists and
turns. What invisible hardships preempted their visible good fortune?

We can only take one day at a time, resting in the fact that the seasons
of life unfold as they should. What is supposed to be will be, so apply
yourself to the day at hand and make it the best you can. What do you do
when unfulfilled desire burns in your chest? What do you do when the
absolute opposite of what you dreamed or expected has happened? What
do you do when those around you are seemingly trying to kill your dream,
destroy your spirit, and upset your faith? Dare to hold on and trust God's
perfect timing. "For the revelation awaits an appointed time; it speaks of
the end and will not prove false. Though it linger, wait for it; it will certainly come and will not delay" (Habakkuk 2:3).

➤ LOOKING INWARD ◄

- What unexpected developments have upset your hopes?
- Describe how you pictured events unfolding. Was that realistic?
- In all honesty, are you really ready for what you want?
- In what ways can you adjust your expectations? What can you
  learn during this time?
- How might knowing that this season will eventually pass affect the
  choices you make in the midst of it?

➤ LOOKING UPWARD ◄

"There is a time for everything, and a season for every activity under
heaven" (Ecclesiastes 3:1).

WAIT IT OUT

Eventually even well-meaning friends have no more to say. At times, the most profound statements are formed out of their helplessness: "Listen to this, Job, stop [stand still] and consider God's wonders" (Job 37:14). Amen to that! Those were the wisest words spoken out of thirty-four chapters of rehearsing, rationalizing, and speculating the reason for Job's present woes.

Truly there is a time to speak and a time to be silent (Ecclesiastes 3:7). What more can be said when all has been explored and you are still found wanting an answer? It is time to be silent, to wait, and to allow the events of life to unfold in perfect order. Circumstances have a way of falling into place when left to settle on their own. The more we mess with the contents of our life, the more jumbled they become. But taking one step at a time and stepping where you *can* step while you patiently wait for a better season can take you a greater distance than staying stuck on one spot, like a broken record, reliving your disappointment over and over again. Ever notice there is no movement in life when we do this?

Throw up your hands. Let it go. After you have done everything that you can do, stand still (see Ephesians 6:13). When the battle becomes too big for you to handle, that's a good thing. That means it's not your war to fight; the battle belongs to the Lord. Your situation is an opportunity for Him to show off on your behalf. Simply take your position, stand firm, and see the deliverance the Lord will give you (2 Chronicles 20:17).

What exactly does that mean? If I'm supposed to be still and wait, what should my position be? The answer almost sounds too simple: "Wait for the LORD and keep his way. He will exalt you to inherit the land" (Psalm 37:34). The only leg you have left to stand on is your right position in relationship to God. You've got to join the psalmist in saying, "Let integrity and uprightness preserve me; for I wait on thee" (Psalm 25:21, KJV). That is what will preserve you when everything else in your life is spoiled. God will honor your consistency. "Stand in awe, and sin not: commune with your own heart upon your bed, and be still" (Psalm 4:4, KJV). Wait for the promptings of that inner voice known as "something" to some. Those in the know have come to understand that "something" is actually "Someone"—the Holy Spirit relaying God's advice to you. This voice will not shout above the din of confused friends or disconcerted victims. Therefore be still.

When Job came to this place, an incredible thing happened. "Then Job answered the LORD: 'I am unworthy—how can I reply to you? I put my hand over my mouth. I spoke once, but I have no answer—twice, but I will say no more.'... Then the LORD spoke to Job out of the storm" (Job 40:3-6). This statement is mentioned twice: "The LORD answered Job out of the storm" (38:1). Some translations say "out of the whirlwind." The Lord broke through the raging storm in Job's soul and appealed to his spirit. And as God's truth broke through the whirlwind of opposing thoughts in Job's mind, it finally brought him to a place of peace, reconciliation, and, more important, restoration of all he had lost.

But this came only after Job was completely stripped of himself, all the way down to his understanding of life as he knew it. Stripped of his ideas about God's character. Of his self-made plans and all his intricate safety measures. This is a humbling place, after learning so much, to realize we know absolutely nothing! After planning so carefully, to have everything we dreamed of come to nothing but a mess on our hands! How ironic that we find ourselves coming full circle after all is said, done, and concluded, to hear ourselves saying something as basic as "Lead me in thy truth, and teach me: for thou art the God of my salvation; on thee do I wait all the day" (Psalm 25:5, KJV). "You are my help and my shield" (see Psalm 33:20).

That's it. It kills us to say that we can't really help ourselves. We are helpless! Ugh! Yet that's exactly what God is after, killing everything in us that tries to replace Him. All the pieces of us that strive to set themselves up as gods on their own. It won't happen. Forget about it. I can't namby-pamby around with you. Whether you want to deal with God or not, you can't get past Him. Your efforts to figure things out and fix your life on your own will be dismantled time and time again until you come to the end of yourself, until you get out of the way and allow Him to rise to the occasion and glorify Himself by delivering you. While you are waiting for your breakthrough, God is waiting for you to give Him the chance to do the miraculous in your life. To deepen the reality of who He is and the sovereignty of His awesome power to do with you what He pleases. To transform you for *your own good* in order to bring you to the place that *you yourself* ultimately desire to arrive at. So "be still before the LORD and wait patiently for him" (Psalm 37:7).

➤ LOOKING INWARD ◄

- What are you still trying to fix about your situation?
- What scares you about waiting? Why?
- What do you think God is trying to purge from within you?
- What personal idols are being dismantled in your life?
- How is your image of God changing through this trial?

➤ LOOKING UPWARD ◄

"Wait for the LORD and keep his way. He will exalt you to inherit the land" (Psalm 37:34).

When Life Destroys
Your Dreams

He was young, handsome, and single, with huge potential. He was the "Golden Boy." The favored son. He had big dreams. God-given dreams. He was voted "Most Likely to Succeed." Yes, he was definitely going places. But sadly, he wasn't going where he thought he would be going. You see, people don't like dreamers. Telling others of his dreams only won him the jealous response, "Who does he think he is? I think it's time we cut this guy down to size. He wants to go places? Then we'll help him go!" When people don't like you, they hurt you. If they don't actually hurt you, they simply won't help you. Jealousy makes for an ugly enemy. So those he should have been able to trust the most sold him down the river, so to speak, dusted off their hands, and said, "Good riddance."

Suddenly, this young man with the bright future found himself deposited in an unfamiliar place where no one knew who he was. Among people who looked down on him on a good day. Pressed into menial labor, working a job that was definitely beneath his qualifications. So goes the story of Joseph in the book of Genesis. Some know him because of the Broadway musical *Joseph and the Amazing Technicolor Dreamcoat*. But the story of his life is no musical fantasy. It was very real. His trials were beyond imagination.

We can all relate to being stuck in a situation that we don't like. Singleness. Unemployment. Debt. A serious health condition. A bad marriage. The crush of being victimized by someone else's jealousy, divisiveness, or just plain old bad decisions. Of having our good plans go horribly awry.

Of being plummeted from popularity to obscurity. Of working a job we hate. Of feeling that we are qualified for a better position. We've experienced the pain (as the old spiritual goes) of being lied on, cheated, talked about, mistreated. Nothing stings worse than being a victim of circumstances or of someone hateful. After all, if you contributed to your problem, you could at least admit you invited the trouble. But when you *didn't*—well, that just takes the pain to another level of *ouch!*

What do you do when all that you perceived of your fabulous future goes up in smoke on a humbug? When life takes you down and you're struggling to get back on your feet, it may seem you'll never hold your dreams in sight again. But like Elijah, Job, David, and others, our friend Joseph did several things right when things went wrong on his way to becoming the Egyptian Pharoah's right-hand man. And his dreams, because they were ordained and fulfilled by God in His perfect time, *did* come true.

PART III

GETTING BACK ON YOUR FEET

M y t h
Life should be good to good people.

➤ ➤ ➤

T r u t h
Dear friends, do not be surprised at the painful trial you are suffering, as though something strange were happening to you. But rejoice that you participate in the sufferings of Christ, so that you may be overjoyed when his glory is revealed.

1 PETER 4:12-13

KEEP YOUR HEAD ABOVE WATER

The first thing I think we wonder when bad things happen or we hit the unexpected twists in the road of life is, *Where is God?* Yet the text in Genesis 39 says that when Joseph's brothers sold him and he was taken down to Egypt to work in the house of Potiphar, one of Pharoah's officials, the Lord was with Joseph. So much for the theory that if God is in your situation, you won't have any troubles. Where was God? He was right there! When the wind was tossing around the disciples' boat, where was Jesus? Walking on the water to meet them. He even invited Peter, an ordinary fisherman, to come walk with Him on the water too. Peter did—that is, until he became absorbed with where he was. Then he started to sink in his own fear and unbelief.

We are all called and equipped to walk on water, so to speak, the troubled waters of our lives. But if we look down at our state of affairs, we will sink. As long as we keep our eyes up, locked on the Author of our faith, we will overcome. If we are able to take a deep breath and say, "This is only a test," we can apply ourselves to finishing the course.

We can either roll over and die a slow, painful death while repeating the mantra, "Why me? Why me?" or we can rise to the occasion. Realizing I have an invisible enemy who wants me to cave in is usually enough to make me perk up and decide I won't give him the satisfaction of my demise. It's easy to say things can't get any worse, but the truth of the matter is that they can. I recall a particularly bad year in my life when everything that could go wrong did. I would say with each new setback, "Things couldn't get any worse than this." And then things would get worse. Again I would say, "Things just couldn't get any worse." And then they would. About the fifth time I was tempted to utter these ill-fated words, I caught myself. "Things couldn't get— Oh, never mind!"

Wallowing in what can't be fixed has never fixed anything. Don't go there. Instead, I suggest you take God's advice:

> Awake, awake, O Zion,
>> clothe yourself with strength.
> Put on your garments of splendor,
>> O Jerusalem, the holy city.
> The uncircumcised and defiled
>> will not enter you again.
> Shake off your dust;
>> rise up, sit enthroned, O Jerusalem.
> Free yourself from the chains on your neck,
>> O captive Daughter of Zion. (Isaiah 52:1-2)

Now let me break that down to Michelle paraphrase. "Snap out of it! Push out of your fog and buck up! Don't wimp out. Flex some muscle, locate your power, and use it. Fortify yourself with your faith in God and with what you've learned. Purposely put your best face forward even if your insides don't match your outward expression. Those who have unclean motives and lack integrity won't have access to hurt you again. Get over the past. Shake off the bad influences and people who cling to you but are not contributing to your progress. Pull yourself together. Climb above your situation and gain a new perspective. Mark your territory and claim your spot. Free yourself from whatever is hindering you from moving without restraint."

Notice that the people of Jerusalem were given the work of freeing themselves. No fairy godmother was going to show up to free them. How do you free yourself? By embracing the truth and wielding it like a weapon. If the truth is what makes you free, then what is true? God is still on the throne. You are still standing. Therefore there is hope. Deal with your attitude.

When you take stock of your life not at eye-level but at faith-level, you will find something good to work with. Something great to hold out for. Something that will give you the strength to grit your teeth and hang on. Take note that God has been faithful so far. Though you may not feel your best, you are, in fact, living above the circumstances. This is just a test. You are still standing. The rest hinges on your own determination and the decisions you make as you move forward. The old saying "I felt sorry for myself because I had no shoes until I saw a man who had no feet" makes an important point. If you take the time, you will find you have something inside of you that you can use to float until the waves subside and a more solid horizon comes into sight.

➤ LOOKING INWARD ◄

- What about your situation causes you to feel as if you are drowning?
- What foundational truths can you float on at this time?
- What can you do to strengthen yourself? What can you put on to cover yourself?
- What victories can you take back from the enemy of your soul?
- What positives can you find in your situation right now?

➤ LOOKING UPWARD ◄

"Because of the LORD's great love we are not consumed, for his compassions never fail" (Lamentations 3:22).

LAY ASIDE THE FORMER GLORY

Poor Joseph! He went from a house where he *had* servants to a house where he *was* a servant. Dwelling on this fact could have really set him back. If he had chosen to buck the system he found himself in, he could have suffered even more. Yet he chose to play with the cards that had been dealt him. No one cared about or acknowledged his past. Today was a different day, and he was where he was. Imagine an old, faded movie star who still expects to be recognized. More tragic than the faded glory is the time warp he is stuck in, paralyzed by dreams of days gone by that no one else can recall.

Dealing with the present is a decisive battle in winning the war. When we look back we tend to romanticize the past, making it far more glorious than it really was. The present will never measure up. Such backward glancing leaves us to wallow in our misery and lose the ground we need to make progress.

The fact of the matter is that what you were yesterday won't work today if you're not in that position any longer. The urge to scream, "Don't you know who I am!" prevails, but we must stifle that cry and deal with what is at hand. Imagine my shock as I jumped into a cab one afternoon and recognized the driver as a top producer I had worked with for many years. He sighed, "I have been avoiding this street for months, afraid of picking up someone who would recognize me. But I have a family to feed…" I tipped my hat to this man for swallowing his pride and doing what he had to do. To try to assert his past over his present would have been fruitless. To sit in a chair at home and refuse to do anything other than what he had always done would have put him and his family in dire straits. In spite of how you feel about your past and present, think of others. They are relying on your survival so that they, too, might have faith to make it through their own situation.

Consider the wife who must look into the disrespectful eyes of the woman who has taken her husband and face the mutual friends who have grown distant because of their discomfort. Or the fallen CEO. The athlete who was once a legend. The person who has lost a loved one to death and can't let go. These men and women cannot expect the same treatment or experiences they once were accustomed to. Life as it was is forever changed. Whatever the former position and comforts you had, they must be laid aside. You must adopt what is *now*. You must make changes to accommodate your present dwelling until you can move to a better neighborhood.

It is safe to say that Jesus had His moment. After all, when He prayed for the disciples and the rest of the world in John 17, He said, "Father, I want those You have given Me to be with Me where I am, and to see my glory, the glory You have given Me because You loved Me before the creation of the world" (see verse 24). Certainly Jesus longed for those who had walked with Him in His lowly state to see the full picture of who He really was. There was nothing about His present state as a man to suggest His former position as an exalted heavenly monarch.

Jesus' earthly status did not at all negate who He had been, but He had to function in the now. So did Job. He who suffered and lost so much before God restored him, sighed in the midst of his torment:

How I long for the months gone by,
    for the days when God watched over me,
when his lamp shone upon my head
    and by his light I walked through darkness!
Oh, for the days when I was in my prime,
    when God's intimate friendship blessed my house,
when the Almighty was still with me
    and my children were around me,

when my path was drenched with cream
>and the rock poured out for me streams of olive oil.
When I went to the gate of the city
>and took my seat in the public square,
the young men saw me and stepped aside
>and the old men rose to their feet....

Men listened to me expectantly,
>waiting in silence for my counsel.
After I had spoken, they spoke no more;
>my words fell gently on their ears.
They waited for me as for showers
>and drank in my words as the spring rain.
When I smiled at them, they scarcely believed it;
>the light of my face was precious to them.
I chose the way for them and sat as their chief;
>I dwelt as a king among his troops;
>I was like one who comforts mourners.

But now they mock me, men younger than I,
>whose fathers I would have disdained to put with my
>>sheep dogs....

They detest me and keep their distance;
>they do not hesitate to spit in my face.
>(Job 29:2-8,21-25; 30:1,10)

We can all relate to this yearning when we're going through the worst of it. All Job could do was take comfort in his own innocence and God's knowledge of it and then ride out his present trial. And that, my friend, is all you can do. If you insist on your old way of life, the new and better way will elude you. I suggest you use your disappointments as steppingstones to greater undiscovered territory. Lay aside the former glory, file it as a pleasant memory, and await a greater light.

➤ LOOKING INWARD ➤

- What things or persons from the past are you clinging to?
- Why does looking back keep you from moving forward?
- What can you do today to improve your situation?
- What frame of mind about your present circumstances can you adopt to empower yourself?
- What comfort can you find for today?

➤ LOOKING UPWARD ➤

"See, I am doing a new thing! Now it springs up; do you not perceive it? I am making a way in the desert and streams in the wasteland" (Isaiah 43:19).

LET GO OF WHAT
YOU'RE USED TO

Joseph had to relinquish the life of privilege he had formerly enjoyed in order to get on with the business of living through his unfortunate circumstances. As we learn to let go of the past, we must also learn to let go of other hindrances to our progress that weigh us down. Burdensome thoughts. Negative thinking. The desire to control things we cannot change. These things won't help us get back on our feet.

When Elijah found himself hiding out on a mountaintop, he discovered that God wanted him to rise to a new level of understanding.

> A great and strong wind tore into the mountains and broke
> the rocks in pieces before the LORD, but the LORD was not
> in the wind; and after the wind an earthquake, but the LORD
> was not in the earthquake; and after the earthquake a fire, but
> the LORD was not in the fire; and after the fire a still small voice.
> (1 Kings 19:11-12, NKJV)

This is not what Elijah was used to. He had grown used to mighty displays from God. A still small voice was not what he expected. So many have made a religion out of seeking signs and wonders, much to God's frustration. I imagine He sits in heaven, saying, "Noooo, this is not how our relationship is supposed to go! I don't want to always have to be 'on' with you. I'm not always going to show up the same way. I am a God of variety. I will not be boxed into elaborate displays. Sometimes I just want to be able to talk softly to you, to whisper words of comfort to you, to have a real conversation with you. Come on, Elijah. This is just Me and you. There is no one around watching. You have nothing to prove to Me. You're not promoting My cause right now. Let's get real. Why are you here?"

As we often do, Elijah struggled to get past where he was. "I told You, God! I've been working for You, and now people are after my life." *What is it about my situation that You do not understand, God? Why don't You just kill the people who are causing problems for me? I've seen Your powerful displays. I know what You are capable of. All it would take is one zap from You to straighten this out.* We might not say that, but that's what we're thinking. Come on, get honest now!

But God is not concerned about those people. They will get their comeuppance in time. Right now, in this intimate place, He is only concerned about you. How you deal with where you are. What your attitude is. Will you trust Him no matter what is going on? Do you believe that all things work to the good for those who love Him? If you are truly in relationship with Him, then what is the problem? He has your back covered. All you've got to do is keep moving forward with your ears open. You will hear a voice behind you saying, "This is the way; walk in it" (Isaiah 30:21). Just follow the directions and you will find yourself back on track, heading toward the victory no matter how far away that might seem.

But first you must learn to let go of the familiar. Stay flexible and open to change. "But God told me to stand here!" you insist. That doesn't mean it was His intention for you to stay there forever. Things have changed, therefore *you* must change. God's knowledge is too vast to be stuck in one mold. So life pulled a switch on you. He knew it would. So He's ready to introduce you to a new way of life that will accommodate the change. God is "the same yesterday and today and forever" (Hebrews 13:8). This verse speaks of His character, not His methods. He is not a stagnant God. Stagnant waters lead to certain death.

And yet God never wastes any of your discomfort. In fact, He wastes nothing. Good or bad. It's all good if you allow it to be. Obviously life is getting ready to be very different for you. That means that God will have to do something new too. Don't look for Him to do things the same way again, but expect Him to come through nonetheless. Consider this an exciting adventure. Take a deep breath and let go of what you're used to.

➤ LOOKING INWARD ➤

- What old things are you trying to hang on to?
- Describe how God dealt with you in this type of situation in the past.
- What word did He give you at the beginning of your circumstances?
- Are you open to a change of direction?
- Do you believe anything good can come from this change in your life?
- What scares you about change?

➤ LOOKING UPWARD ➤

"But one thing I do: Forgetting what is behind and straining toward what is ahead…" (Philippians 3:13).

BE EXCELLENT
NO MATTER WHAT!

Speaking of getting over what you're used to, our misplaced friend Joseph worked his new role as a slave to his advantage. He left everything he touched in a better state than it was before. Soon Potiphar elevated Joseph to the role of personal assistant and gave him authority over everything in his house except his wife and what he chose to eat. You see, Potiphar noticed that the Lord was with Joseph and blessed everything he did. Something about Joseph's disposition suggested he could be trusted. Imagine what would have happened had Joseph remained disgruntled and performed his duties with an attitude of forced obligation. We would never have heard how his story ended. He would have been written off as a malcontented slave, never entrusted with more than menial tasks.

I can't say whether Joseph was *happy* about his situation, only that he made the best of it. After all, it wasn't Potiphar's fault that Joseph was where he was. Joseph wisely didn't project the hard feelings due his brothers onto his boss. Instead, he strove to be excellent and fruitful in Potiphar's house.

Our position in life does not define our character. How we handle our position does. A queen deposed is still a queen if she was a queen inside. A brilliant man who loses his job is still a brilliant man. Likewise, Joseph's handling of matters in Potiphar's house proved he was no ordinary slave. Potiphar chose to acknowledge the statement Joseph's life made, much to his personal gain.

Others' responses to us are reactionary, and so excellence begets respect (though sometimes grudging), no matter what the initial opinion might have been. This is why God says we should work hard and cheerfully at whatever we do, as though we were working for the Lord rather than people. Remember that the Lord will give you an inheritance as your reward and that the Master you are serving is Christ (Colossians 3:23-24). I believe in most cases this applies to now as well as the hereafter.

By following the same principles, four young Hebrew men—namely, Daniel, Shadrach, Meshach and Abednego—rose to power in Babylonian society. Because of their obedience to God and their devotion to excellence in all things, He gave them the gift of wisdom. Their brilliance elevated them above the cultural perception of where they should be placed. And more impressively, an entire book in the Bible is named after a captive. Because he was a captive in title only. Their story is told in the book of Daniel.

What you bear within will determine your outward title. I once interviewed a man who was then CEO of the McDonald's corporation. He started off serving fries. He applied himself to serving them with a smile and being excellent. He knew this was a temporary position. He saw potential in himself and eventually became what he saw.

I also think of a woman who was born physically handicapped to schizophrenic parents. Struggling to maintain her sanity while living on the streets, she managed to acquire a scholarship to Yale University. This woman who lived in a storage bin while attending school with the crème de la crème of society kept pushing onward and upward. No one knew what she was going through, but that wasn't important. In her mind she was going *through;* she wasn't staying. While struggling to get around the campus, which was not handicap-accessible then, she became instrumental in changing not just her own situation but also the situations of individuals with physical limitations who would follow. Today Yale is handicap-accessible because of this one woman who could have allowed her circumstances to make her believe she had nothing to contribute to society. She turned her pain into a weapon, and her victory was not merely personal. It improved the quality of life for others.

Fight the urge not to do your best because you are not where you want to be. Stop being mad at God and others. No matter how disgraceful your situation, be a lady. No matter how emasculating, be a man. Observers will have to give you credit.

Also, ask God for creative ways to get back on track with your life. Ask Him to bless all that you do so that you can rise to the top of your situation. It has been said that our mess becomes our ministry. Our test becomes our testimony. But only if we grasp it firmly and make it work for us. This means charging through the center of your pain and not changing your standard for getting the best and the most out of life. You will get back to that if you persist. Besides, the best revenge against an enemy, visible or unseen, is success. So be excellent, no matter what.

➤ LOOKING INWARD ➤

- What is your present attitude toward applying yourself with excellence? Do you believe the potential outcome is worth the effort?
- Are you striving to function at your maximum potential now? Why or why not?
- What things in your life have you let slide to a mediocre state? How can you change your attitude in those areas?
- What is your motivation for wallowing in self-pity? Does it bring anything positive your way?
- How could your excellence make a greater impact on those around you? your own state of mind?

➤ LOOKING UPWARD ➤

"In the same way, let your light shine before men, that they may see your good deeds and praise your Father in heaven" (Matthew 5:16).

MAINTAIN YOUR INTEGRITY

Pain is the ultimate test of character. It whispers seductive suggestions to you in the night. Things to get you off your square. To pull you off course. To delay your comeback. Destructive but tasty enticements to fluff up your flesh and cater to yourself. *After all, you deserve it. You've been through enough.* Go ahead, have a piece of chocolate. Take that petty cash from the till. Drown your sorrows in that bottle. Avoid people who make sense. Find friends who commiserate with your self-destruct—I mean, self-indulgence.

Joseph found himself facing such an invitation from Potiphar's wife. If he had not already built his spiritual house and stayed focused on his dreams, Joseph might easily have given in to the temptation. The English translation of the woman's words reveal an ironic truth about her proposition: "Come and lie with me, Joseph" (see Genesis 39:7). Truly, intimacy without covenant is merely a lie. It holds no promises of tomorrow, only the temporary gratification of the immediate moment. The consequences don't reveal themselves until later in all variety of destructive forms. All temporary self-gratification is that way. From telling a little white lie to overindulging in food or alcohol to losing yourself in drugs to chasing lovers. Whatever soothes the wounded beast within you when you are in pain is merely a mirage of a better day. It won't get you there; it ultimately offers only greater pain.

Joseph wasn't going for it. And it wasn't because he was afraid of being caught either. He said, "How then could I do such a wicked thing and sin against God?" (Genesis 39:9). *Forget the consequences. Forget Potiphar. Forget you, lady! Your rejection complex is not what I'm worried about here. I am concerned about being true to my God and true to myself. I never was and never will be a man who delights in covert activity.* Are you? Yes, I am talking to you. Who were you before your trial began, before pain opened the door to temptation? Find that person inside and stay true to him or her.

"He or she made me do thus and so" are famous words. But they are not true words. No one can *make* you do anything. Other people's invitations and encouragement can only reveal what is already in your heart. Who are you really? Proverbs 30:20 tells us that the adulterous woman wipes mouth and says she has done nothing wrong. That's because she genuinely believes she is right. This conclusion reveals a lot about her character. She has no concern for others. That means her willing lover will suffer betrayal at her hands as well. It is her nature to fulfill her own needs without caring what it costs anyone else whether male or female. We are all true to our own nature, whether wrong or right. The source of your temptation is irrelevant. Don't let your ego lie to you. The invitation you received has been and will be given to others.

But back to Joseph. He did things to ensure his integrity. He set boundaries. Which suggests that he knew he had weaknesses. He didn't resort to gossiping about it. After all, whom could he tell? He remained silent and held himself accountable by avoiding Potiphar's wife as much as possible.

"It just happened" is a contradiction against the power we have over ourselves. *Nothing just happens.* Too much goes into committing a deed. Too many steps are taken when the opportunity to turn back is at hand. The body obeys the mind. If the mind is not made up ahead of time, the body has no defense but to follow through on its present desire for gratification. The body does not consider the future. The mind does. Therefore consider the invitation of the flesh.

Having an affair. Seeking revenge. Lying. Overeating. Indulging in harmful substances or behavior. Robbing someone emotionally or materially because you feel you have been robbed or violated. *Whatever.* These are not conducive to long-term peace and fulfillment. Do not compromise your ethics. Remain in a place where you can be transparent.

Hide nothing. Be honest about your weaknesses. Set boundaries for yourself. Stay accountable to someone who can guide you without condemning you. Do whatever it takes to resist the urge to grab temporary relief. Hold out for lasting security. The desire will pass. The consequences will not.

➤ LOOKING INWARD ◄

- What standards did you live by before your trial?
- Describe how your trial has changed the standards you now live by.
- What hard-to-resist invitations have presented themselves?
- What boundaries can you set to stay grounded in the right way?
- Are you willing to be held accountable? Why or why not?
- Who and what are most important in the scheme of how you want your future to unfold?

➤ LOOKING UPWARD ◄

"I have hidden your word in my heart that I might not sin against you" (Psalm 119:11).

FIGHT THE URGE TO BLAME

When things don't go the way we like, our first instinct is to blame someone for our mess. Sometimes it *is* someone else's fault, but as I mentioned in chapter 1, more often than not the culprit lies within. Yet the shame of our failure or disappointment causes an automatic reflex, and we've got to divert the blame. It is too heavy a load to take on ourselves. It hurts too much to raise our hand and admit, *Hey, this is of my own doing. My mouth got me in this mess. I failed. I missed it. To be perfectly honest I have no idea what just happened.* And so we blame others. The devil. God.

I find two profound phrases in the book of Job. The first is "In all this, Job did not sin by charging God with wrongdoing" (Job 1:22). Is it sin to blame God for the fallibility of humanity? I believe it is. The other remark is from Job himself, who came to a conclusion of immense maturity: "Blessed is the man whom God corrects; so do not despise the discipline of the Almighty" (Job 5:17). Wow! Who has ever welcomed a spanking or a rebuke and termed it good medicine? Yet Job had a point. No suffering could be as great as the pain of being disowned by God and never being pulled up short. In His love He, the best of parents, allows life to teach us valuable lessons and shape our character. Some psychologists call this "tough love." Indeed God's love is tough, and it is enduring.

I once heard a parent say as she spanked her child, "This is going to hurt me more than it's going to hurt you." I'm sure the child couldn't see the logic of that at all! And as that parent administered correction with tears streaming down her face, I knew her heart was breaking. She was the source of pain to one she loved, yet she knew a greater pain would await the child if she didn't teach him that there are consequences for rebellious actions.

When people are buffeted by life in terrible ways, God stands weeping over His children. "Precious in the sight of the LORD is the death of his saints" (Psalm 116:15), whether that death be physical, emotional, or spiritual. Your pain is His; He grieves both the pain that is necessary and that which is not.

When Stephen, a steadfast believer who proclaimed the gospel, was stoned to death for defending his faith, Scripture says that Jesus stood up at the right hand of God, so filled was He with compassion for what was happening to His beloved servant (see Acts 7:55-56). He did not stop Stephen's death, but He was there, arms open wide, ready to receive Stephen into heaven and into the joy of a rest we have yet to comprehend. In our selfishness we see death as the final period at the end of the sentence of life. To God it is merely a comma. Tragedy should also be regarded as a comma, a rest before the push to rise above where you are. Tragedy pushes us out of our comfort zone. It says, "Hey, wake up! Pay attention to this area of your life. Don't stay here! It's not good for you."

Whether we would like to admit it or not, placing blame is a way of abdicating responsibility. It takes the focus off our part in the unfolding drama and keeps us from admitting our own shortcomings. Like Adam, when confronted by God after disobeying His specific instructions, we point our finger and say, "It was that person that You put in my life. And you know what? It's not just that person's fault, God, but it's Your fault too, for allowing him or her to be there to influence my behavior." Such excuses didn't hold water with God then, and they don't now. Adam still had to pay the consequences for his actions, and so do we.

Why waste the blame when you can use the pain? Joseph did not dwell on the betrayal of his brothers and blame them for the hardship he suffered. He embraced his trials and got the victory. Job didn't blame God—and neither did he blame the devil! Now isn't that interesting? It was actually the devil who had not only instigated this mess but also carried out Job's devastation! Yet he was not a factor for Job. Why? Because Job was too busy with self-examination, looking for any open door that could have invited his bleak circumstances. When he found none, he stood firm in his convictions that no, he would not insult God. He fought the urge to cast blame and instead let the true culprit be dealt with in time.

➤ Looking Inward ✦

- Do you take responsibility for your own life, attitudes, and actions, or do you tend to look for scapegoats?
- Describe how blaming others in the past has affected your progress through trouble.
- Do you avoid deep introspection on a regular basis?
- When God disciplines you, what is your reaction?
- Are you open to God's correction? Explain.

➤ Looking Upward ✦

"You intended to harm me, but God intended it for good to accomplish what is now being done" (Genesis 50:20).

REMAIN GRACIOUS

The woman was downright mean. Mean and nasty. There I was, a customer, paying for *her* services, and she was treating me—*not* happily—as if she were doing *me* a favor. As I started to ask for the manager to complain about her inappropriate demeanor, an inward check made me take a deep breath and say something else: "Are you having a bad day? You seem to be in distress about something." Well! What did I say *that* for?! She burst into tears and released an avalanche of personal tribulations. I ended up counseling her and praying for her before I left.

What if I had been having my own bad day and had been insensitive to her? What if I had gotten caught up in my own emotional reaction to her nastiness? On top of what she was already experiencing, I would have added to her trauma by getting her into trouble at work.

As hard as it may be, no matter how great your stress level, remain gracious. The same people we meet on our way up, we will inevitably meet on our way down—and up again, and down again. Such is the cycle of life. And if you are on that downward slide, keep in mind that other people you meet are not the problem; they are probably just as out of control as you are. In times of personal panic, it is hard to discern who is friend and who is foe, who can help us and who might hurt us. So take a deep breath and guard your reactions to those around you.

Who could've been a more gracious host than Joseph when his deceitful brothers ended up in Egypt looking for food? He was free to be so because he had come to learn that they were not his problem. They were merely pawns in the hand of his ultimate destiny.

Surely Job could have gone off on his faultfinding friends as they bombarded him with suggestions of all that he had done wrong to earn his predicament, yet he did not. In the end, when God showed up on the scene to give His opinion, He basically said they *all* were wrong. Even so, He didn't allow Job to stick out his tongue and say, "Nah, nah, nah, nah, nah, you sorry so-and-sos! I told you so!" On the contrary, God told Job to pray for his friends. Pray that they never have to go through what you went through. Pray for their lack of understanding. Pray that they will get the same revelation of Me that you now have because of your experience. After all, that was what the whole exercise was about.

Now some might say, "That was very cruel of God. Why didn't He just tell Job what He wanted him to know?" But the truth of the matter is that we are hard of hearing in most cases. Second, God knows that we are an experiential people. We can hear something all day long, but when we experience it, then we *know* it to be true. So just settle it within yourself that the testing of your faith develops perseverance. Let perseverance finish teaching you those hard lessons so that you will develop a deeper maturity for facing future dilemmas. (See James 1:3-4.) As we go through this life, its highs and lows should no longer cause our emotions to rise and plummet so drastically. Your psyche should become more stable with experience. Now *that* is true maturity. Your growth is dependent on your ability to "keep your head in all situations [and] endure hardship" (2 Timothy 4:5).

Your endurance is the most effective way to communicate the faithfulness of God to those around you. Because believe me, they are watching. Freaking out does not make God look good. It only makes people question what you stand for—or why you're not standing if you truly trust the One you claim to rely on.

Paul, the writer of most of the New Testament, understood this principle. He wrote this to those who watched him go through persecution, beatings, and even jail for his faith: "If we are distressed, it is for your comfort and salvation; if we are comforted, it is for your comfort, which produces in you patient endurance of the same sufferings we suffer" (2 Corinthians 1:6). In other words, if you can watch me go through these things well, when you go through similar circumstances, you will remember my endurance and believe that you will make it too. People constantly seek reassurance through the victorious examples of others.

Yes, God allowed Joseph to be betrayed, Elijah to be threatened, Job to suffer loss, but it was not because He didn't love them. No, quite the opposite. God permitted their suffering *because* He loved them and considered them to be His sons. He trusted them to handle their problems the right way. He counted on their power of endurance. They all learned valuable lessons from their experiences. Job in particular learned a few things about himself, discovered a side of God he hadn't known, and realized he couldn't formularize his relationship with God any longer. God is bigger than all our preconceived notions of how to "manage" Him. He will not be contained by our formulas and prayer mantras. God is sovereign. He does as He pleases. And we are surprised to find that we, too, are pleased. "Endure hardship as discipline; God is treating you as sons [or daughters]. For what son [or daughter] is not disciplined [or taught] by his father? If you are not disciplined (and everyone undergoes discipline), then you are illegitimate children and not true sons" (Hebrews 12:7-8).

But back to Job's friends. God said to Job, "Be nice to them. Just because you had it half right doesn't give you a license to beat them up and become self-righteous. See their need and pray for them."

This is a big principle, because we will only get as much mercy as we give. Forgive so that you yourself can receive forgiveness. If we treat others horribly, in our time of need we will be kicked while we are down. Those we offend wait to kick us when we're down, and they rejoice in our misfortunes. Job humbly prayed for his friends, and their relationship was healed. His attitude cleared the playing field for Job to be blessed. I find it interesting that Jesus instructs us to reconcile our broken relationships and forgive the offenses of others before we try to give offerings to God (Matthew 5:23-24). Bitterness leaves no room for God to bless us. We curse ourselves by hanging on to the past and bring disease to our own spirits by refusing to let go of old, unhealthy stuff.

Isn't it interesting that after Job prayed for his friends, his fortunes were restored double? His prayer for them released them to bless him, because there were no old accounts left unsettled between him and his friends. I'm sure they were willing to help Job in the rebuilding process of his life because they had nothing against him.

When King Abimelech took Sarah into his harem, thinking she was Abraham's sister, God took away the health and fertility of the king's wives and concubines. When Abraham retrieved Sarah, God told him to pray for the king and his household, and the Lord restored their health. Catch this: *After* Abraham prayed for them, Sarah became pregnant. God fulfilled Abraham and Sarah's long-awaited promise after a difficult act of obedience. (See Genesis 20:1–21:2.) Even Jesus had to pray for His enemies before He could be glorified. There is something to be said for keeping your decks clear with people and being gracious at all costs. It can't hurt you one bit. But it can help you beyond measure.

➤ LOOKING INWARD ◄

- Have you caused others to bear the brunt of your pain?
- What hurtful words have you said to others? What were the effects?
- Are you willing to forgive those who have not been as understanding toward you as you would have liked them to be?
- What negative behaviors have you allowed to pile up in your personal relationships?
- How has holding on to old offenses made you feel? Has it hindered your growth in any way? Explain.

➤ LOOKING UPWARD ◄

"Let your conversation be always full of grace, seasoned with salt, so that you may know how to answer everyone" (Colossians 4:6).

WHEN LIFE ROBS YOUR PEACE

♛

She was a good woman, a good girl from a good family. They had chosen her husband carefully, making sure their daughter was married to a man who could provide for her in the way she was accustomed to living. Though they were a little concerned about his family name, they didn't dwell on it long; his credentials were outstanding. He was wealthy and seemed suitably enamored of their daughter. So they trustingly gave him her hand in marriage.

She was genteel and kind and beautiful. Her mother had raised her well to be a good wife and a wise woman. But her task grew more difficult with every passing day as her new husband lived up to his name. The man was a fool. There was no other way to say it. A complete fool. Bad tempered. Arrogant. Inconsiderate. Loud, abusive, and disrespectful. Everyone lived in fear of him and dared not challenge him on any point. Imagine her shock and disappointment. Most women grow up expecting to meet their dashing prince, their knight in shining armor who comes to carry them away to the land of love and marriage soon to be followed by the baby in the baby carriage. But that was not to be the case for her.

Instead, she found herself waking up next to a man who changed like the wind. An ogre. Erratic and moody. Everyone around him was trained to step lightly. She was no exception. She fought the urge to shrivel up inwardly. To allow him to change her would be an even more unbearable way of life. But what was her recourse? Fools make foolish decisions that affect everyone around them. One foolish person can put an entire household in jeopardy. Ruin finances, psyches, and even long-term security. Fools make enemies. Enemies strike back and are no respecters of persons when they do. The fool and his household become one in the eyes of the enemy. This is what the life of this woman came to one day. How could she circumvent the ruin her husband had invited on them all?

David, the anointed king of Israel, had been hiding in the desert from the reigning King Saul. David had run low on supplies, so he sent messengers to Nabal, the wealthiest man in the region, to ask if he had any provisions to spare. David's men had protected Nabal's shepherds and flocks when they were last in David's territory. But Nabal insulted David and refused to give him anything. David was angry and threatened to destroy all that belonged to Nabal. A servant escaped the skirmish to let Abigail know what was going on. Abigail kept a level head and saved their household—more on those details later. Such is the lot of those who have a fool in their lives. They toe a fine line between surviving and triumphing. In this case, Abigail triumphed.

Sometimes life won't wait for us while we wait for it to smooth over. Sometimes we must make decisive and strategic moves to secure our well-being—even our very lives. Let's follow the lead of Abigail and let her quick wits and her triumphs be our example.

PART IV

STANDING FIRM

M y t h

Life should stick to your agenda.

➺ ➺ ➺

T r u t h

Many are the plans in a man's heart, but it is the LORD's purpose that prevails.

PROVERBS 19:21

REMEMBER WHO YOU ARE

Beware the fools who enter your life. The danger of spending too much time with a fool is that it heightens your chances of becoming one too. If you're not watching, some people will take you there. To Fool City, if you know what I mean.

Don't allow yourself to be pushed there. Perhaps your situation is more dire than being influenced to do something foolish. Perhaps you feel bound to someone whose very character is dominated by a nature that is not conducive to peaceful living. Poor Abigail. Abigail was married to a man named Nabal who was such a fool that he ultimately endangered the lives of everyone in their household. Do you know anyone like that? She could not reason with her husband, so she had to take matters into her own hands before they were all destroyed. One of her servants noted that she was the only one he could talk to. Obviously she was able to maintain the reputation of being a wise and reasonable woman in spite of her foolish "other half."

Abigail did not become a fool with Nabal. She saw him for what he was and did not allow him to change her. Although she was his wife, she maintained her own character apart and separate from him. How critical this daily choice proved to be in the hour when she most needed wisdom! And how critical a choice this is for those of us whose troubles are caused by fools.

Decisions have to be made when you are dealing with a fool. Who were you before this foolish episode began? Maintain that spirit. Maintain and strengthen it by gaining wisdom. You can gain wisdom by, for instance, watching a fool. After all, a fool can teach you all the things *not* to do. A fool's mouth brings him to ruin. Therefore measure your own words. A fool has no rein on his anger. Master the art of self-control. A fool is wise in his own eyes. Gauge the reactions of others to your behavior and don't fool yourself. A fool repeats the same mistakes over and over again. Learn your lesson. A fool is quick to argue. Don't go there! Arguments are the beginning of many battles you will lose because a fool is never finished being foolish.

In the presence of a fool, it is important to remain clear on who you are. For example, I was recently experiencing an excruciating toothache that seemed to spread throughout every filling in my mouth. I thought I was going to have to have every tooth refilled! But my dentist explained to me that only one of my teeth was behind all my discomfort. He went on to tell me that the mouth is very sensitive. When one tooth suffers, it transfers pain to the rest of the mouth. That's kind of what happens when you live with a fool, an alcoholic, or an abusive person. It's easy to become an enabler. To take the blame for their wrongs. To get used to their foolishness, even accept it. Living with a fool can become "normal" if you let it. After a while you will begin to believe their madness is sanity and accept it as such, never realizing you are in a hazardous place.

Abigail did not. Just as Joseph maintained his integrity in the face of extreme temptation, Abigail maintained what she knew to be true about herself in the face of her husband's foolishness. She was not about to allow herself or all that she held dear to be destroyed. She did not seek to shield Nabal from the consequences of his actions, but she did move to protect the innocent. She would not cower and be a victim. She would not make excuses for his bad behavior. She would not cover for him or go into denial. No, she would do what she had to do to secure the household's well-being, and she rose to the occasion.

It is said that a wise woman builds her house, but a foolish woman tears it down with her own hands (Proverbs 14:1). She tears it down by the things that she does or says. Although I am sure in many cases Abigail felt that her husband was tearing down the walls of security in her life, she chose to build her house by firmly establishing the foundation of her own character. Scripture tells us that the woman called Wisdom built her house on seven pillars: prudence, knowledge, discretion, counsel, sound judgment, understanding, and power (Proverbs 8:12-14; 9:1).

Let's consider what this story means to you. You have to exercise caution when you're dealing with a fool. Foresight is of paramount importance. You have to stay one step ahead of the game and, based on your knowledge of the fool's character, anticipate that person's next move. No room for denial here. Gather information. Know what and whom you are dealing with, and accept the information at face value. Don't hope for something different. It is what it is. Then exercise discretion. Not everyone is going to understand and know how to deal with your situation. Bad advice from the wrong source can be your undoing. Weigh the advice you receive, and exercise good judgment before you make a move. Understanding exactly what your options are and what is realistic in your situation will empower you to move forward. Fortify yourself. Don't panic, react impulsively, or give in to the wave of foolishness. This will take great discipline on your part. So take a deep breath. In with the good, out with the bad. Stand firm, and collect your thoughts. Quietly build up your strength from within, and maintain who you were before this all began. Though Abigail had suffered long with Nabal, the one thing she did *not* suffer from was an identity crisis.

➤ LOOKING INWARD ➤

- Has the fool in your life made you lose sight of who you are?
- Do you find yourself feeling responsible for that person's behavior?
- Do you go into denial or try to avoid the issues you have with this person?

- What does this person cause you to question about yourself? Are those questions valid?
- In what ways have you changed since being with this person? Is that change good or bad?

➤ LOOKING UPWARD ◆

"Do not answer a fool according to his folly, or you will be like him yourself" (Proverbs 26:4).

Be Resourceful

Poor Abigail! Not only was she married to a fool, but she lived in a society where it was not acceptable for her to leave her husband. The fact of life for her was that she had to buck up and deal with her present circumstances. The present demanded action. Abigail could not sit around wallowing in disappointment or embarrassment over her husband's outrageous actions. Lives were at stake, and she could not trust Nabal to come through with a solution. She gathered her wits about her and got busy. You have to be creative when you are dealing with a fool. Resourceful. You've got to be able to pull not just *yourself* together, but other people and whatever else is needed to ensure the well-being of your personal world.

How do you do that? First, by knowing that you are not your own source of strength, sanity, or provision. You have someone on your side to help you through. Your mind-set has to be, "I have set the LORD always before me. Because he is at my right hand, I will not be shaken" (Psalm 16:8). Now that that is established, count to ten, exhale, and do whatever your hands find to do. In other words, do what you can and expect God to back you up.

Abigail knew that she could only do one thing at a time. She didn't have time to chastise Nabal about his foolishness; that wasn't going to change anytime soon. Instead, she chose to tackle what she could handle. She dealt with the immediate crisis. Her husband had offended someone who needed provisions. All right, that was simple enough. She gathered together all the rations she could and set out to meet the irate David, who was on his way to her house with murder in his heart.

Perhaps in your case debts are soaring, creditors are calling. Don't run and hide. Calmly deal with each one. Talk to people. See what compromises or arrangements can be made. Most of the time people are nice when they know you are trying to do *something*. They cannot help you if they don't know you need help and are willing to be cooperative.

Abigail did not settle into self-pity or get defensive. She simply did what she could do, and if that wasn't good enough, well, she would have to rely on the grace of God. Truly in our weakness He proves to be strong. He will take up our part as we learn to lean on Him, not as a crutch but as an able partner in our mishaps.

In the end, if you have a relationship with the One who made you and treasures you, He will not allow your demise. He will defend you because you belong to Him. The battle is not yours. It belongs to the One who is able to fight and win on your behalf. He simply asks that you show up on the battlefield with what you have. And one of the most overlooked gifts that we have is the gift of negotiation. We simply don't use it enough because we don't believe we can pull it off. Why? Perhaps we don't really trust God to give us the favor we need. We've had too many previous disappointments. Throw that score sheet out. That was then. This is now. You are equipped with more knowledge.

Begin where you are with what is at hand, and build from there. If all you have are words, then carefully use the power of those words. If you have a little something that you can offer to smooth out the situation, use that. Be flexible in finding solutions to your problems. Research new sources. Just don't give up or give in to the impending threat of disaster. Ask for help. Don't isolate yourself. Don't resort to pride and secrecy. Neither will help you. Draw what you need from others to get through. Strength. Advice. Encouragement. Material needs. Whatever. There is strength in numbers.

Abigail rounded up the members of her household to help her pull together everything she needed and set out to see if she could appease David—not to cover for Nabal, but to secure peace for all who would be affected if she did not. Now was not a time for her to get upset or to hide behind her shame. At times like this a person has got to do what a person has to do. Abigail did not hope that Nabal would come to his senses or that David would change his mind. But she calmly confronted the situation head on. And in the end, as you will see later, it paid off royally.

So do what you can do. Simply take what you have, lay out there, stand still, and see the salvation of the Lord. God is the greatest resource of strength and wisdom you can have in times like these. He is faithful to send help from His sanctuary and support from Zion (see Psalm 20:2). So be resourceful. Draw what you need from Him as well as from those He sends into your life, and then use what He provides.

➤ LOOKING INWARD ◄

- How does panic manifest itself in your life when your well-being is threatened?
- Do you fall apart or become supernaturally focused when under pressure? What determines your response to tests?
- Should outward circumstances be able to affect you inwardly? Do they? If so, describe how.
- What sources can you draw from to maintain calm?
- What do you control in your circumstances? How can you use it to secure yourself?

➤ LOOKING UPWARD ◄

"I can do everything through him who gives me strength" (Philippians 4:13).

STAND IN THE GAP

I often say that, when dealing with human beings, we must keep in mind that people are only able to do what they can do. They only know what they know. Expecting them to do or know any more will only frustrate us. To try to change them is even more exasperating. It won't happen. Only one Person can change people. The Holy Spirit. If we are always vocally challenging the person who causes difficulty for us, we drown out the voice of the only One who is able to change minds and hearts. We cannot be anyone's Holy Ghost. The only person we have control over on any given day is ourselves. Therefore, talk less and pray more. Pray for that person.

God expects those who are stronger to bear the infirmities of the weak, which is exactly what He does for us. Jesus stood in the gap for us between the anger of a holy God and our naturally sinful state. Because of His self-sacrifice, we have access to God. Jesus became the connection that made us friends with God when we were unable to do it on our own. His example does not mean that we should saddle ourselves with everyone else's "stuff" and become a victim. It means that we should lift them up as much as we can through encouragement, patience, and intercession. Interceding means that you make a plea to God on their behalf, mediating in a sense between them and the One they probably will not approach on their own, out of either fear or ignorance. You literally stand in the gap for such people, filling in the great divide between them and the help they need. You become the bridge that helps them to cross over if they respond.

Now let's talk about the difference between standing in the gap and getting in the way. Rescuing a person from his or her bad or codependent behavior is definitely getting in the way. People who never experience the consequences of their actions begin to believe there aren't any. This is not good. In the end, they meet a tragic end as their bad behavior and foolish choices go unchecked. That is why God allows us to be caught by our own mistakes. It is His way of correcting our behavior and training us to grow up in integrity. He disciplines everyone He loves. Yet some of us have this twisted concept that, if we really love people, we should let them get away with murder. In they end they do; they kill *you*, either emotionally or physically.

But if I don't take care of this or that, they will face an incredible loss! Let them face it. Perhaps loss will be their gain in the end. Never make life easier for a fool. He will take it as a reward for his folly. In the meantime, get out of the way, stand in the gap, and pray. If the fool's folly has an immediate effect on you, then you must weigh whether the matter is life-threatening. If it is, take action.

In Abigail's case, her husband's folly had greater consequences than outstanding debt. Because it had created a matter of life and death, Abigail went to David and literally absorbed the blame for her husband. However, she did not cover for him! Scripture tells us that Abigail was an intelligent and beautiful woman, and her intelligence shines through her words to David. (See 1 Samuel 25:24-31.) She told David she was to blame *only because she didn't know what had been going on.* If she had known what he had requested of Nabal, things would never have escalated to this emotionally charged level. She admitted that her husband was a fool and encouraged David not to allow Nabal to upset him. In essence, she said to David, "Why lower yourself to his standards? He always was and always will be a fool. You are not. Don't allow him to pull you below your personal standards."

Abigail reminded David of the big picture. He was destined to be a king. Therefore, he didn't have time to be a fool. It was not in his best interests. Because she had lived with a fool, Abigail was able to recognize the difference and see the potential for foolishness in others. So she spoke to the king in David and dismissed the fool that he could have become in a fit of temper. She spoke reason to his spirit, his inner man, and he responded to her wise counsel. She provoked his sense of decency and appealed to the better person within him. There is something about the words "You are better than that." These simple words can reveal what really lives in the heart of a person. If the person is indeed not a fool, the challenge will cause him to take the high road. Such was David's case.

This little lady didn't flinch in the face of this angry man. After all, she was used to anger. She understood it and carefully defused it. Now was not the time to point out David's own foolishness in considering retaliation. She lifted him up instead. She rebuilt the part of him that Nabal's caustic words had torn down. She took him off the defense and released him to maintain his dignity in a situation where his manhood had been threatened. She was a wise woman. Her wisdom appealed to his, and the gap between them was closed.

When you are in the position of interceding for the very people who would bring harm your way, you have to humble yourself and appeal to the higher nature of the person who holds the key to your solution. In this respect God and man are alike. They both resist the proud. But those who are humble find grace extended to them. They move hearts to sympathy and hands to helpful action. When you feel helpless, humble yourself under the mighty hand of God, and He will lift you up and come to your aid. Make an appeal. Bless your fool by praying for him or her.

Pray strategically. Ask God to do whatever it takes to bring about a change in that person's life. Pray that He will break the yoke of foolishness from their lives. Now, there's a scary prayer! But it's a necessary one, and you must be ready for whatever happens. No matter what happens next, fight the urge to rescue your fool. Simply continue standing in the gap and watch. Watch and pray good confessions over the person. Decree the person they can become by the transforming power of God. Watch and wait until they cross over to the other side and the gap between you closes.

➤ LOOKING INWARD ◄

- Have you been trying to convince your fool to be otherwise? What have the results been?
- What can you do to put out some of the manageable fires in your life?
- In what areas do you need to stop rescuing your fool?
- What is the best way you can stand in the gap for your fool? What is your prayer strategy?
- Have *you* ever been the fool? Who and/or what helped you snap out of it?

➤ LOOKING UPWARD ◄

"We who are strong ought to bear with the failings of the weak and not to please ourselves" (Romans 15:1).

PICK YOUR BATTLES

When keeping the big picture in mind, you have to let some little things slide. After all, nitpicking your fool will not get you the results you're after, just as tracking every offense will only keep you spinning in the same spot. You've got to remain sensitive to God's grander scheme and pick your battles. Give careful thought to your ways and the tendencies of the person you are dealing with. Don't repay anyone evil for evil. Sometimes it's better to just go your way and let the chips fall where they may. Don't get caught up in the madness. "Be careful, or your hearts will be weighed down with dissipation, drunkenness and the anxieties of life, and that day will close on you unexpectedly like a trap" (Luke 21:34).

Most people have a tendency to act out when under stress, but it is important to keep allies. Make sure to "do what is right in the eyes of everybody" (Romans 12:17). Be faultless and rally the right support. "Be very careful, then, how you live—not as unwise but as wise, making the most of every opportunity, because the days are evil" (Ephesians 5:15-16). Hold tightly to that big picture. Discard your tendency to grasp for immediate gratification and short respites. Although you might have good cause to holler, don't become like the boy who cried wolf. Eventually your cries will fall on deaf ears grown used to your voice. Therefore, pick your battles carefully.

When Abigail returned home from her dramatic encounter with David, her husband was having a party, oblivious to their close brush with death. Having a party! Can you believe it? The average person would have stomped into the room, turned off the CD player, and sent every guest packing. Then the real fireworks would begin. The fool would be confronted and, as they say in Urbanese, it would be *on!* But Abigail was not your average person. She went to bed and let him finish partying. She waited until the next morning before calmly telling Nabal what had happened the day before.

Do you know that the fool had the nerve to be *upset?* We're surprised, but I'm sure Abigail was not. That is exactly why she hadn't bothered to share the details with him until some time had passed. If she had told Nabal that she intended to take food to David, she wouldn't have made it out the front door. Calamity would have struck and devastated them all. If Abigail had told Nabal about her encounter with David when she returned home that night, Nabal probably would have sent his men to confront David and retrieve what Abigail had given them. That, too, would have been an ugly sight. So she waited.

Sometimes we feel the need to let a fool know that *we* are not a fool. That is a wasted exercise. You are asking for a fight. It is not an important point to prove when so much else is at stake. Simply consider your options and move with deliberation. Timing is crucial. "A man's [or woman's] wisdom gives him patience; it is to his glory to overlook an offense" (Proverbs 19:11). Abigail knew that "the end of a matter is better than its beginning, and patience is better than pride" (Ecclesiastes 7:8) and that only "through patience a ruler can be persuaded" (Proverbs 25:15). Patience gives you a gentle tongue that can break down the hardest of hearts.

The choice is yours. Insist on winning every little battle and lose the war, or hold your peace and wait for the big bomb to drop. I do not advocate divorce, but sometimes separation is essential to personal safety. If your situation is abusive and beyond your ability to endure, and you feel you need to leave it, don't give in to the urge to explain why you are leaving. Don't try to make the fool see the error of his ways as you depart. It won't matter to a fool; you will never be right. Also, don't try to get compensation for your hardship; your life will only become harder. It is best to make a peaceful, quiet break. Risk is always a part of trying to take your life back from the hands of fools. They are prone to retaliation.

Abigail had taken a risk. A *necessary* risk, but a risk just the same. The revelation of what she had done had to be timed carefully. Though she had taken matters into her own hands and appeased someone who could have become an enemy to them all, she still had to live with Nabal. Yet, since she had tapped his resources, he could not afford to keep her action a secret. So she waited for the appropriate time when things were quiet and all other distractions had ceased.

Baby! The man got so upset that he had a heart attack! Really! He had a heart attack and fell into a coma. Now, that is what anger unchecked will do for you. It will take you out of here. Better him than her in this case. And the story doesn't end there. Not only did he fall into a coma, but he died several days later!

I daresay that Abigail had not expected this, and we don't know her reaction to this turn of events, but I am pretty sure of one thing. She had a clear conscience. She had done the best she could. She had done all the right things, and Nabal's blood was not on her hands. His foolishness, and his foolishness alone, had paved the way for his early demise.

I'm sure there was some dancing and singing going on a stone's throw away from Abigail by those who had also been oppressed by Nabal's folly. *Ding, dong the witch is dead!* In the minds of many was the resounding conclusion that Nabal had gotten exactly what he deserved. But I imagine Abigail grieved the loss of a life that didn't have to be that way. Perhaps in her own wise way she understood that in the heart of every fool is a wounded child who never gained enough understanding to reconcile his pain. In light of that fact, it didn't matter who was wrong or right. It seemed trivial to add injury to insult by scolding or correcting one whose already shattered psyche made him incapable of absorbing another blow. Therefore Abigail chose to hold her peace and pick her battles.

➤ LOOKING INWARD ➤

- Are you able to release the offenses of your fool, or do you harbor them? Give an example.

- Do you feel the need to make a point every time your fool does something you don't like or approve of? What is his or her response?
- How do you feel when your correction is ignored or ridiculed? Does that reaction help the situation? Does your attitude worsen or improve?
- What would give you more peace in this situation?
- What keeps you from being more patient and discerning about the best timing for your confrontations?

➤ LOOKING UPWARD ◄

"Thus saith the LORD unto you, Be not afraid nor dismayed by reason of this great multitude; for the battle is not yours, but God's" (2 Chronicles 20:15, KJV).

LEAVE THE REST TO GOD

At times during your journey, you will not know how to proceed. When in doubt, do nothing. Wait for clear direction.

But what if God gives none? This simply means there is nothing for you to do. As one pastor used to say, "When you don't know what to do next, keep doing the last thing God told you to do." Whatever else needs to be done, He will do it. That is a scary thought for many. *Uh-oh! What is God going to do? Is He going to do something with my life that I don't like? After all, up to now, the events of my life are not what I would have selected from a list of options. If He has already allowed me to go through such excruciating trauma and drama, will He hand out more of the same? I don't know if I trust Him with my life anymore.*

That's interesting. When you thought you were in control, did things go any better? I can tell you the answer: No. True, the problem with leaving everything up to God is that nothing is in your control. And yet, when we finally come to the end of ourselves and let go, He surprises us with joy. He surprises us with things better than our eyes have ever seen, our ears have ever heard, or our hearts have ever imagined. God's imagination is incredible. The most amazing thing is that He knows what we want and need even better than we do. And when we least expect it, He comes bearing an unbelievable package filled with all our heartfelt desires and dreams come true.

Now is the perfect time to tell you the rest of Abigail's story. When David heard about the death of Nabal, he sent for Abigail not just to offer his sympathy, but to offer his hand to her in marriage! Isn't that something? One day she's married to a fool; the next day she's married to a king. And you thought that only happened in fairy tales. Now, I can't promise you that God will *kill* your fool. He might just kill the fool *within* him or her (or you), allowing the king or the queen to emerge. Only God can exchange your fool for royalty. But only you can yield your life to His principles for living. I don't know when He will turn things around in your life, but His promise is sure: He will.

What is your responsibility in this? Wait on God and persevere. If you can stick it out and stand the test, you "will receive the crown of life that God has promised to those who love him" (James 1:12). That crown of life is full of all the things that make life worth living: peace, joy, fulfillment. So many people bail out of their situation before the breakthrough comes. And then the haunting questions begin to assault them. What if I had waited? What if I had done this? Or that? But there is a liberation that comes when you know you have done all that you can and you have been supernaturally delivered from your pain and rewarded for your endurance.

Let me insert a brief note for those who find themselves in situations of life-threatening abuse. As I mentioned earlier, one must exercise wisdom. Get help. Remove yourself from danger. In some cases these relationships can be rectified, but usually only after the person is sobered by the reality of loss. Distance does not prohibit God from fixing things. Stand back and let Him handle it.

Otherwise, when life seems hard and you see no light at the end of your tunnel, keep walking. Keep believing that your diligence will make a difference. One theologian tells this story of his own folly: At the time, he was not a Christian, although he was married to a godly wife. He despised her relationship with God and tried everything he could think of to destroy it. At every turn, he thwarted her efforts to attend church. He locked her in rooms and hid her shoes. One evening when she went to church, he locked her out in the cold until the next morning. She patiently waited for him to open the door in the early dawn. Her only words were "And what would you like for breakfast?" Her love penetrated his cold heart, and once he came into his own relationship with God, he went on to revolutionize the Christian world with his teachings. Think what the world would have been robbed of if his mistreated wife had not stood fast and clung to her belief that God was able to do what she could not: change her husband's heart.

Many of us miss life's payday by quitting in the middle of the job. I often hear from wives who have incredible husbands: "Oh, honey, he wasn't always that way. We had to go through the fire to get where we are in our relationship now, but it was well worth it." I think Jesus says the same about us: "Oh, honey, I had to die for that one, but it was worth it." What made Him stick it out with a group of twelve guys and a ragtag band of followers who rarely understood what He was talking about? The knowledge that eventually they would get it and that their understanding would revolutionize the world.

Nothing worth having comes in a hurry. Remember those wine commercials? (I may be aging myself here.) "We will sell no wine before its time." Some things just need to sit and ripen. Nothing is done to the liquid left fermenting. The course of nature does its own work to perfect the wine. And, true to the story of the wedding feast when Jesus turned water into wine at the end of the party, God always saves the best for last. (See John 2:1-11.) We must simply be willing to wait for it and not interrupt His work.

So take the pressure off yourself to do the impossible. Where would you begin anyway? It's time to open your hands. Not in defeat, but in expectation. You've done your best, and it's all right to confess your weariness. Take a clue from Abigail. All she *could* do was all God asked her to do. He took care of the rest.

➤ LOOKING INWARD ➤

- What has God asked you to do? Have you done what He's asked?
- Are you trying to do things God has not asked you to do? What are those things?
- Does giving up control of your situation frighten you? Why?

- Do you trust God with your life? Where have your best efforts gotten you?
- Have you been in God's way? Explain.
- What will you stop doing so that God can begin fixing your situation?

➤ LOOKING UPWARD ◂

"You will not have to fight this battle. Take up your positions; stand firm and see the deliverance the LORD will give you" (2 Chronicles 20:17).

When Life Takes What Is Dear

♛

He was tall, dark, and handsome. A foreigner. She always found a certain...*intriguing* mystique about those who came from faraway places. His way with her was different from what she had observed of the interaction between men and women in her land. She had dreamed of a man like this. One who made her feel beautiful and desirable. And here he was, asking for her hand in marriage! Dreams of "to have and to hold forever, amen" filled her every waking thought as she prepared to be his bride. It was almost too good to be true. She must have held her breath until the final vows were spoken lest even exhaling should wake her from her dream.

She knew his parents did not exactly approve of their son marrying a woman who was not from among their own people. But perhaps in time they would get used to the idea. Sure enough, and much to her surprise, his mother warmed and treated her with a kindness she had not known even from her own mother. The two women grew close over the years, and in time she followed her mother-in-law's example of how to be good wife.

But then a villain entered this perfect little tale. Cancer. It knocked her handsome prince from his horse with one fatal blow. She cared for the one who had cared for her until their perfect love story faded to black before her very eyes, and death claimed him.

Her grief was more than she could bear. Her own husband's death had been preceded by the deaths of both her husband's father and his brother. These losses had taken a toll on the family emotionally as well as financially. Not only did she have to deal with the reality of being alone, but she had real concerns about her financial future as well. Life as she had imagined it was over. This was not a nightmare she would wake up from. This was real life. In living color. All she could do was adjust the hue.

As she struggled with her own emotions, she watched her mother-in-law and sister-in-law with grave concern. Her mother-in-law was growing more bitter by the day. What had she done to deserve the death of her husband and sons? Where was God? How much crisis was a person expected to endure at a time? How ironic it was that they had moved to this country to avoid death—times were hard in their homeland—only to learn that they could run but couldn't hide. When it's your time, it's your time. But why did it have to be time for all three of them? Wasn't that a bit much? The more the old woman pondered every point of her misfortune, the more bitter and inconsolable she became.

As for her sister-in-law, she mentally closed shop and withdrew. Her eyes were vacant, as if she had left the building of her soul, deciding there was no reason to stay around.

Though a widow herself, the young woman watched the grief-stricken women around her and decided there had to be something to live for. Now was not the time for her to become lost in her pain. She must be strong for those who were weak. She would have time later to ponder how her promising future had been so cruelly interrupted.

But before she could act on her thoughts, she found her mother-in-law packing. Packing to return to her country. The older woman would make one last attempt to reconnect with the familiar. How ironic, the daughter thought, that she would long for something new while her mother-in-law reached toward her past for comfort. As she began to help her companion in grief gather the last of her belongings, she made a difficult decision. She would accompany her. Her mother-in-law's old comforts would become her own new beginning. Her mother-in-law feared dying alone. She feared being trapped in a hopeless present. Perhaps together they could find new hope.

WHEN LIFE TAKES WHAT IS DEAR 141

As they started off down the road, her sister-in-law began to weep. As always, her mother-in-law was sacrificial, urging the young widows to return to their childhood homes. There was no need for them to go with her, she said. There was no hope for them where she was going. In her land, foreigners were not exactly embraced, and they would not have a good chance of finding new husbands. They would be better off staying behind. Although her sister-in-law was swayed and turned back, the young woman thought differently. She would not be dissuaded. It would have been easier not to move on, but move on she would. Toward what she knew not, but she would find out soon enough.

The woman I am speaking of is the legendary Ruth, a Moabite. Her grieving Israelite mother-in-law, Naomi, headed back to Israel after the death of her husband and two sons. This was a risky journey for Ruth. Yet even as she headed toward a land that was hostile toward her people, she remained resolute. She was driven on by an inner determination that her past was not her future. She would not be bound to her present. She would reach beyond where she was and embrace a new beginning, no matter how painful the initial effort was. And so she uttered the words to her mother-in-law that have become famous: "Where you go I will go.... Your people will be my people and your God my God" (Ruth 1:16).

Wow! Ruth was willing to not only change her location, acquaintances, and allegiances, but she was willing to adopt an entirely new belief system. And she was absolutely adamant about her decision. She could not be swayed to deviate from her course by any person or circumstance, even while her companions attempted to discourage her.

When you are bowed down with grief, what are you willing to do to get your life back on track? Some abdicate the reins of their lives when they find themselves in this place. Though there is a time to grieve, there is also a time to make critical decisions about tomorrow. What will you choose when you can't see tomorrow through your tears? Where will you find the strength to stand firm in your decisions? Ruth shows us the way by her example. Let's follow her lead.

PART V

LETTING GO AND MOVING FORWARD

M y t h
Life should get easier as it goes along.

➤ ➤ ➤

T r u t h
But if you suffer for doing good and you endure it, this is commendable before God. To this you were called, because Christ suffered for you, leaving you an example, that you should follow in his steps.

1 PETER 2:20-21

KNOW WHEN IT'S OVER

The hardest thing for many of us to do is to know when it's time to cut our losses and move on. We think, *But I've put ten years of my life into this relationship, into this business, I've got to make it work. It can't be over just like that!* Why not? What's the saying? "All good things must come to an end"? They don't have to, but sometimes, unfortunately, they do. Does clinging to a dead thing bring it back to life? No, it only paralyzes you. If you cling too long, in fact, your heart will become diseased by the deterioration of what you refuse to give up.

I was once deeply in love with a man, and we planned to spend the rest of our lives together. But he was suddenly killed, putting an end to my dreams. I never got to see him dead (he was cremated), which robbed me of the closure I needed to deal with a fact I did not want to accept. For years after I could still be jolted by seeing someone who looked like him. My unwillingness to release him kept me in bondage—unable to get on with my life and be open to another relationship. Ruth had to deal with watching her husband suffer and die. There was no denying that her life would never again be as she once knew it. She was forced by the finality of it all to move on.

One day Jesus was talking to the disciples about not being too attached to things and situations. One of them said to Him, "Lord, let me go and bury my father first before I go with you." Jesus replied, "Let the dead bury their own dead" (Luke 9:60). Now, that might sound a little cold and unsympathetic, but He was actually saying, "Don't let the death of what is dear to you keep you from moving forward. Don't miss the invitation to be blessed and to be a blessing because you are too distracted by something you can do nothing about." It is necessary to know when it is time to move on.

Before Jesus ascended to the Father after the Resurrection, He told the disciples, "Don't cling to me. I have to go, but I will send you a Comforter." I'm sure He was warmed by the fact that they wanted Him to stay. I'm sure He even reflected on how much He was going to miss these men. But Jesus could not just consider His own pleasure. It was time to go. It was a new season. For Him to remain would have hindered their growth. He made a sacrifice for the greater good. With Him gone, they would be forced to grow up in their faith.

I've met many who struggle to get over the death of a loved one. Years later they are still talking about the loss as if it occurred yesterday. Such behavior is a disservice to the one who has gone on. Yet some seem to think they honor that person by continuing to grieve over him or her. It would be far better to create a personal ritual for saying good-bye, acknowledge the good the person brought to your life, and then, in honor of that person's memory, get on with the business of living. Become a living memorial that would make the person smile if he or she could see you now. What better way for Ruth to honor her husband's memory than by taking care of someone dear to him: his mother.

The same principle applies to mates who have left. Positions that have been terminated. Dreams that have died. Take the time to formally say good-bye in your spirit. Remember the good times and place them in your spiritual photo album. Cut the cord. Dive back into life. That is not being cold or unfeeling. It is simply necessary. Life is for the living. To stop moving is to die.

So that plan or relationship didn't work out. It is time for a new one. The possibility remains that the opportunity might be revived. But let go and give it the chance to do so on its own.

I have a little mantra I use when things don't go as I think they should. When the situation is wrong and you are wrong, God says *no*. When the situation is right and you are wrong, God says *grow.* When the situation is wrong and you are right, God says *slow.* When the situation is right and you are right, God says *go!* That about sums it up. God's prevention is His protection. Resist the urge to see the departure of a loved one, whether by death or choice, as abandonment. Consider that person's situation and acknowledge what he or she might have been going through that brought things to this end. Then ask God for the grace to release the one you loved. Leave room in your conclusions for the things that you do not know.

This applies not just to the death of a loved one, but also to the death of any situation in our lives. We lose the victory we could have when we refuse to accept change by focusing on what *has* been—what we no longer have or have never had. One-tree-itis. Um hmm. That's what most of us have. We get stuck on the one tree we can't eat from. Yet we are standing in the middle of a garden that offers a bounty of luscious fare. Life offers us so much that we never partake of when we choose to be prisoners of our own pain. Our insistence on having what we want gets us in trouble, hung up, stuck every time. In Urbanese it's called being "stuck on stupid." It is stupid to beat a dead horse. The horse is not aware of what we're doing. It cannot respond. We exhaust ourselves to no avail.

It's time to give it a rest. Don't talk about it. Don't revisit it anymore. It's over. To refuse to face this fact is like not accepting that summer or winter is over and refusing to wear the right clothing. Not only will you look ridiculous wearing a coat in ninety-degree weather or summer apparel in below-zero temperatures, but you will either burn up or freeze to death. It is unhealthy not to embrace change and make the necessary transition. Now is the time to focus on an important issue: What do we do next?

Until you face the reality that this season of your life is over, you will be unable to plan your next move. Rebuild your future according to a new plan. At the end of his ministry, Elijah, who had definitely recovered from his depression, told Elisha he was going to be leaving. He had come to the end of his road and was ready to be with God. The others in the school of the prophets started hanging back, not really wanting to deal with what would happen after Elijah was gone, but Elisha started making plans. He did not reserve the hope that something different would occur. Such reservations put a person in a holding pattern. Hoping against hope. When Lot and his wife were told to leave Sodom and Gomorrah in Genesis, they were also told not to look back. Poor woman clinging to the past, she took one last longing glance back and was turned into a pillar of salt. Forever frozen in time, unable to move on with her life. What if Ruth had not moved on, deciding to stay in Moab to be rescued by one of her own people? She might have missed out on gaining a wealthy husband, and she certainly would have missed out on being included in the lineage of Christ!

False hope keeps you from taking another, or better, opportunity because you are bound to your reservations. When Elijah announced that his time to leave this earth had come, his assistant Elisha took what the prophet said at face value. He clicked in to "securing-his-future" mode. If Elijah must leave, Elisha would ask for a double portion of the anointing that gave Elijah power to do miracles. Elijah told Elisha he could have it— *if* Elisha would watch him go up when the chariot of God came to take him away. So Elisha watched. He was willing to press past the painful loss in order to receive what he needed to get on with the rest of his life.

This is a powerful scene! Elijah was saying, "Watch me depart. Face facts. Don't flinch from the reality of what is happening. See it, believe it, and use it to go on. If you can deal with death, you can certainly deal with life and all it will throw at you." Now that's what I'm talking about. Taking the things that were learned when you spent time in the presence of that person. The valuable experience you gained while in that position and using it to keep on keeping on. But first you must be willing to acknowledge when it is over.

➤ LOOKING INWARD ◄

- Have you been able to close the book on your situation? Explain.
- Are you ready to start a new chapter in your life? Describe how you will begin.
- Where do you see yourself going from here?
- What has been the hardest thing for you to face about where you are?
- What plans can you begin to make to secure a better future?

➤ LOOKING UPWARD ◄

"When Jesus therefore had received the vinegar, he said, It is finished: and he bowed his head, and gave up the ghost" (John 19:30, KJV).

KEEP THE GOOD PARTS

Don't throw out the baby with the bath water. Let go of the past, but keep the good memories. Though I finally had to let go of my boyfriend who died, I kept the memory of how much he loved me. If I were never in love again, I knew what it was like to be loved. That was priceless. It was something that could never be taken away from me. It also gave me a standard for my future relationships. I knew what was possible and what was unacceptable. The memories of a good marriage, a job well done, a life well lived are like a great bank account. You can withdraw smiles and comfort for years to come. It is also a rich heritage to pass on to your children.

Ruth decided to keep the good part of her past and to turn her attention toward something she could touch immediately. The good part included happier times she had shared with Naomi, her mother-in-law. Things she had learned from her. Woman-to-woman things. Things about Naomi's faith and simple way of life that had become a source of comfort to Ruth. She clung to these and considered them too good to let go.

Now, I'm not telling you to be strong to the detriment of your emotional health. Go ahead and grieve. The pain will only come back to haunt you until you give in to it and lie broken in its arms. Do not despise being broken, but extricate the good parts from your pain and brokenness. Brokenness increases our value. "How can that be true?" you ask. What good can come out of being broken? Compassion, passion for the causes of others, selflessness, greater character, humility, and finally strength. Over the course of Ruth's story, we can definitely see that all these admirable traits were born in part out of her own suffering.

Think of fine bread with a thick crust. We break this bread so we can get to the good part inside and receive nourishment. There's a great spiritual lesson in that natural example. Similarly, the rose is crushed so we can enjoy its incredible fragrance. Before, it was beautiful to look at, but now we get to share in its beauty by actually wearing its scent. If we left it in its former state, it would have eventually withered and died, fading out of our memories without leaving anything lasting behind. But the oil from its petals becomes a lasting memorial to what once was.

Even Jesus had to be broken in death before salvation could be given to us. So yield to the breaking; it is good. Cry. Reminisce. Allow others to comfort you and help you rise again. Talk it out. Walk it out. Just make sure you make it out. Ask God to reveal the purpose of the gift you were privileged to have for a time, and accept it as such. Let that revelation equip you to embrace your pain for a season. Squeeze it. Learn from it. Drain it dry. Sweep away the ashes, and then commit to seize strength. Strength begins with the decision to cling to the One who keeps it in reserve. In our weakness His strength fills us in ways that will surprise us. Ask Him for His strength, and drink deeply from the cup He offers. It's all good.

Perhaps your situation has nothing to do with a person. Maybe it is a career that has gone south. A financial empire crumbled. What were the good parts? What lessons did you learn? How will you apply them to your future? If you did it once, you can do it again—but this time you'll do it better now that you are older and wiser.

Sometimes in our effort to overcome pain, we erect monuments and smear them, thinking that if the past doesn't look good, then we won't miss it. Not true. Ruth did not claim to have made a bad decision in marrying a foreigner. She didn't wallow in what might have been if she had done something differently. No, she cherished her husband's love and honored the love her mother-in-law had also extended to her. The truth will cry out and remind you of good times gone by.

By the same token, we should not romanticize our past either. But we should keep uppermost in our thoughts the truth that God works all things together for good for those who love the Lord and are selected to fulfill His purposes. That would be you, I presume. Though your past experience was great, there is always something better. God will bring something good out of this if you are open to receive it. Yes, there is life after this. It is waiting for you. So discard what you will not need for the journey ahead, but keep the good parts.

➤ LOOKING INWARD ◄

- Which good things will you treasure from times gone by?
- How can these memories assist you with your future?
- What priceless lessons did you learn from the past situation?
- How will those lessons help you shape your tomorrows?
- Are you able to thank God for the good parts and not blame Him for the bad? What commitment do you need to make to Him at this time before moving on?

➤ LOOKING UPWARD ◄

"And we know that in all things God works for the good of those who love him, who have been called according to his purpose" (Romans 8:28).

LOVE THOSE WHO ARE AVAILABLE TO BE LOVED

Somewhere along the way, Ruth discarded the idea of getting another husband and decided to love whoever was available to be loved. At the moment, it was her mother-in-law. Ruth decided to lay down her own life to serve this disillusioned woman. Ruth no longer had a husband. She didn't even have a child to hold in her arms to preserve his memory and comfort her. All she had was Naomi. And two choices: She could go in search of what she didn't have and stand the risk of never finding it. Or she could embrace the person who was available to be loved right there. Right then.

But we human beings are a funny lot. We want to love whom we want to love, end of discussion! I think of women who worry about the alarms sounding on their biological clocks. My question to them is always, "Do you want to be a mother, or do you simply want a child?" There are children all over the place begging to be mothered—overlooked as many women insist on bearing a child from their own bodies. I believe God's economy calls those who are without to take care of those who already exist and have a need. But in many cases, we overlook this simple truth or decide the option does not fulfill the specifications of our desire, and we kick it underfoot. Motherhood becomes an idol while the motherless are ignored.

Giving of yourself to someone in need is not always easy or pleasant. When you are in pain yourself, it may seem that the last person you'd want to be around is another melancholy person. Yet something happens when you turn to help the needy: You forget your own need. Ruth did not sit down to partake of Naomi's self-pity pie. Ruth allowed her mother-in-law to have that party on her own but stood by to brush away the crumbs she might be tempted to pick up off the floor. Could it be that Naomi's pain distracted Ruth from her own? In any case, Ruth seemed determined to show this forlorn woman that she had a reason for living. So in spite of what abandoning her own desires would cost her, Ruth reached out. And though it didn't seem possible, Ruth was surprised to find in the end that the two of them became each other's support system.

Only in laying down all her dreams about one type of life did Ruth find a life greater than she could ever have anticipated. I won't give away the end of her story just yet, but suffice it to say, it was awfully good.

Though it defies logic, pouring yourself out for the sake of others is always the first step toward finding your true desires. I think of a woman who now hosts a national television show. She had attempted to succeed in show business for many years, only to be disappointed time after time. Eventually she got married, decided to quit working, and invested herself in helping her husband build his career. She ended up doing odd jobs around a television studio part-time while her husband was attending school. She never brought up her former television experience or tried to get a position on camera. She was perfectly happy doing what she was doing, relieved to finally be free of the pressure to compete in that world. One day when a regular host was not available to tape a special segment, the station needed someone to fill in. Someone decided to try her out in the slot. She landed in the center of her dreams without even trying to.

It is almost as if God waits for us to get over ourselves before He gives us what we really want. Could it be that He knows our hearts and our needs better than we ourselves do? Could it be that He knows we are going about getting what we want in the wrong way? Going in the wrong direction? Giving to the wrong person? All the while, He points in a direction opposite what we want and says, "This is the way! What you want is over there!"

But we don't listen. We are so myopic that we fail to see the opportunities for love, success, and fulfillment standing on the fringes of our peripheral vision. So He lets us exhaust our efforts until we finally give up, and He breathes a sigh of relief. Our words "Oh, forget it!" are music to His ears. We are finally out of the way. The coast is now clear for Him to give us the true desires of our heart.

Could it be that our own selfishness circumvents the serendipitous moments in life that God choreographs to our ultimate desire? How profound is the statement that those who seek to save their life will lose it, but those who seek to lose their life will save it (Luke 17:33). The death of a dream or a loved one can tempt us to turn inward, to nurse our wounds, to miss the opportunity to give others what we think we don't have. If we were paying attention, we would discover that we have everything we need to bless others and to receive blessings ourselves.

I think of the widow whose story is told in 1 Kings 17. As she anticipates her death and her son's death by starvation, Elijah the prophet comes by and asks her to fix him a small cake and give him some water. She tells him she doesn't even have enough for her own family. That very day she would fix the last of what they had and get ready to die. But Elijah urges her to fix the cake for him, promising that she will still have plenty left. As she begins to make a cake for him, her barrel of meal and her cruse of oil are replenished to overflowing!

Truly it is more blessed to give than it is to keep seeking to receive. To serve instead of waiting to be served. To do what little you can do without looking for a great reward. It will come.

Ruth left her familiar surroundings, her gods, her culture, and her friends to love one person in a land of strangers. She chose to forget what was behind and strain toward what was ahead. It was not without effort, but she shouldered the challenge and prepared to move forward. She took the risk of loving one person—not her first choice in a perfect world—and soon found herself propelled toward a destiny of joy and fulfillment.

We can all settle into feeling sorry for ourselves. Clinging to the past. To how things used to be or should be. We could dig in our heels and insist that life go our way. Furnish us with what we want. With *whom* we want. We can keep toiling away in search of our ideal, trying to claim that which is not ours until, exhausted, we finally open our hands and accept what is before us. Or we can simplify our life and accelerate our own healing process by loving those who are available to be loved. Even if we don't feel like it.

Press past your own sense of loss. Serve someone. Love someone. The rewards will be endless.

➔ LOOKING INWARD ◆

- Are you withholding love or service from someone who needs you?
- What is keeping you from reaching out to those around you?
- What or who do you feel holds the key to your happiness and wholeness?
- Are you willing to sacrifice what is dear to you in order to gain something greater? Why or why not?
- Where can you begin to invest yourself today?

➔ LOOKING UPWARD ◆

"And live a life of love, just as Christ loved us and gave himself up for us as a fragrant offering and sacrifice to God" (Ephesians 5:2).

Be Prepared for Change

Though we scream long and loud about the changes we want, are we really ready for them?

I'm going to leave Ruth for a few chapters to tell you the rest of Joseph's story. Joseph's little networking experience with the two men in jail—remember those dreams he interpreted?—bottomed out to nothing for two whole years. Although everything he had told them came true, they forgot about him after they were released from jail.

Have you ever felt capriciously poised over the precipice of a great opportunity, only to be dropped into a vat of disappointment as the whole deal disintegrates before your very eyes? You think to yourself, "What in creation was *that* all about? Why would God wave a carrot in front of me and then snatch it back?" The bigger issue is, "Were you ready to eat the carrot? Would you have known what to do with the carrot if you had been able to seize it?" Most of us are quick to say yes until time has passed and maturity has set in. Then we more readily admit that it was best we didn't get what we wanted at the time. I've been there.

Just as you thought you met the man or woman of your dreams, the romance blew up. But later you discover things about that person you never knew while in the relationship. Or how about that business deal that looked so promising? It appeared to be the answer to all your needs and then poof! In hindsight, you see that the business dissolved, and you would have gotten the rotten end of the stick in the deal. Those are just two examples of how God saves us when we don't realize we need deliverance. But how about when we simply are not ready for where we want to go? Sometimes He leaves us simmering longer than we like because He knows we're not done yet.

So Joseph, an innocent man, simmered in jail for another two years. And then one day it happened. The pharaoh had a dream. A dream he could not understand. Didn't I tell you recurring themes unlock the door to your destiny? This is the third dream in Joseph's story, but perhaps the most significant of all. Then Pharaoh's wine steward remembered that Joseph had interpreted his dream in jail. He passed this piece of information on to the pharaoh. Before Joseph could utter, "What's up?" he was yanked out of prison, washed, shaved, and dressed, and he found himself standing before the highest-ranking leader of Egypt!

This turn of events might have left the most outstanding of men dumbfounded, but Joseph was not impressed. After all, God had been preparing him for this day for years, so he took it in stride. Staying in the Spirit kept Joseph from being overwhelmed by this incredible opportunity. Most people in his situation would have quickly blurted out the long litany of misfortunes they had experienced and submitted a plea for help before they were dismissed. But Joseph said nothing about himself or his state of affairs as he stood with quiet dignity before the pharaoh. When Pharaoh told Joseph he needed an interpretation of his dreams, Joseph informed him that God was the interpreter of dreams. Amazing! After all that Joseph had been through, God was still his most prominent and central concern. I believe God honored Joseph's humility and submission. This was the final test that Joseph had to pass. Would he remember God in the face of greatness? Indeed he would.

So many of us get what we want from God and then say, "Thanks, God, I'll take it from here." God will often wait to give until He is sure we won't take our hand out of His and run ahead of His plan. He requires us to stay with Him when the change finally comes. He will not allow the change—the fulfillment of our desires—to overtake our relationship with Him. Joseph passed the test.

Joseph interpreted Pharaoh's dream, made a few wise suggestions about what to do with the information, and immediately found himself promoted to being none other than the pharaoh's right-hand man. Yeah!

Not only was he put in charge of the land of Egypt, but he also got a wife out of the deal. Well! I bet you could have blown Mr. *and* Mrs. Potiphar over with a feather when they got news of that one! Joseph stepped up to the plate and hit a home run.

Many of us grow comfortable in our misery and sabotage our new beginnings. We can't see past where we are, and we are not equipped to deal with the shifting winds that blow our way. But Joseph never resigned himself to his circumstances; he remained in a state of anticipation about what God would do. He determined that things would have to change, and he would be ready when that change occurred.

Are you ready? No matter how permanent and endless your nights filled with weeping may appear, remember that joy comes in the morning and will usher in certain change. Be ready for it.

➤ LOOKING INWARD ➤

- Are you resting in your current situation, anticipating the change that will certainly come, or are you merely resigned to your present circumstances?
- What is your attitude toward your future?
- Are you ready and equipped to deal with the things you want to happen? Explain.
- Can God trust you with those things? Why or why not?
- In what ways are you preparing for change?

➤ LOOKING UPWARD ➤

"Stand firm then, with the belt of truth buckled around your waist, with the breastplate of righteousness in place, and with your feet fitted with the readiness that comes from the gospel of peace" (Ephesians 6:14-15).

Bank on the Future

So what exactly did Joseph say to the pharaoh that impressed him so? Joseph told Pharaoh his dream was a warning of things to come. The land of Egypt would experience seven years of plenty and then seven years of famine. Joseph suggested that Pharaoh store the surplus of crops during the years of plenty so that the nation could eat the reserve in the years when crops would not grow.

In essence, Joseph told the leader what he had learned from his various trials: Anticipate and prepare for the future. The man who finds the inside of his house flooded during heavy rain doesn't just fix the present mess. He realizes that it will rain again and patches his roof while it is sunny. One should never get too comfortable. Save for the future. Not just material things but spiritual strength as well. Make sure your reservoirs are full.

How does this counsel apply to your situation? You should always make sure you have something to draw from during your time of trial. You might say, "Well, it's too late now, Michelle. I'm already in the thick of it." Stop and check again. You have something to draw from: those "good parts" I mentioned earlier. Memories of how God has brought you through. How friends and family were part of previous healing processes. This is probably not your first trial. Examine your trophy case of previous victories in the midst of suffering, and bank on God bringing something positive out of the negative.

No matter your situation, God can resurrect what has died in your spirit. Your joy. Your peace. Your strength. Your realization that He is able to fill the empty spaces. Your understanding that we Christians are passing through this earth on our way to eternity, where we will meet one another again. After the death of my boyfriend, I ran to the arms of God and found greater joy than I had ever known. Without experiencing such intense grief, I doubt if I would have discovered the joy that could be mine. I was too distracted by the present to consider the One who wanted to be present in my life every day.

I recall the first time I fell in love and got my heart broken. I thought I would never recover. And yet I did. As a matter of fact, I fell in love again and concluded that it was better than the first time! When my heart was broken again, I again uttered that I would ne-e-e-ever fall in love again. But I was reminded that I had said those exact words the first time, and things had turned out differently. I learned that the heart is resilient, capable of loving again and again no matter how many times it has been shattered. I've lost jobs before and worked again. I've been broke and recovered financially. Therefore I bank on the future, looking beyond my present. I try to be prepared for setbacks, and when they occur, I recall times that God helped me overcome. This gives me the peace I need to tread water until I get back to more solid shore.

So be full of God's promises. Not in your head, but in your heart. He will hear you. He will deliver you. Those promises will rise up to remind you that everything is going to be all right. After all, keeping your panic to a minimum is important. It frees you from reacting and enables you to respond calmly to the things going on around you.

The apostle Peter offers wise counsel too: "In your hearts set apart Christ as Lord. Always be prepared to give an answer to everyone who asks you to give the reason for the hope that you have" (1 Peter 3:15). What is the hope that you have? That God takes care of those who belong to Him. "Consider the ravens: They do not sow or reap, they have no storeroom or barn; yet God feeds them. And how much more valuable you are than birds!" (Luke 12:24). Valuable indeed! Think how you grieve when family and friends suffer at the hands of life. You strive to find a way to make things better for them. God is like that toward you. Not only will He feed you things to repair your broken heart and shattered dreams, but He will feed you with strength to keep going and with knowledge of what to do to ease your way. New hope. Renewed faith. A support system around you. Material needs. Spiritual reinforcement. Emotional rejuvenation. God desires your wholeness. He will not rest until you are restored.

God, too, banks on the future. In His foreknowledge of all world events, He looked through the window of time from ages past and saw you exactly where you are right now. He prepared provision to help you ahead of time for every area of distress you would ever experience. He is not rocked by the events that have rocked you. He is not amazed by your disappointments. He anticipated them all. God does not snicker at our helplessness in times like these. He is empathetic and very involved in our pain. "As a father has compassion on his children, so the LORD has compassion on those who fear him; for he knows how we are formed, he remembers that we are dust" (Psalm 103:13-14).

That is the heart of God toward us as we struggle in our way. He banks on our weaknesses to give Him the opportunity to do what He does best: work all things to the good. He is faithful. You can bank on that and anticipate a brighter future.

➤ LOOKING INWARD ◄

- What has surprised you about your situation?
- Have you experienced anything similar to this before? What was the outcome?
- What resources do you have to draw from right now?
- Whom would you consider your support network? Have you reached out? Why or why not?
- What truths can you draw upon for comfort at this time?

➤ LOOKING UPWARD ◄

"'For I know the plans I have for you,' declares the LORD, 'plans to prosper you and not to harm you, plans to give you hope and a future'" (Jeremiah 29:11).

LET GO OF THE IDOLS

We all have a portrait of the picture-perfect life. How it should be. Who should be in it. What we should acquire. We spend a lot of time trying to put these pieces in place and make them secure. But what starts off as a natural goal can become an obsession. An idol in our lives. Our struggle to secure what we want, what we think we deserve or find reasonable to expect, overshadows the One who empowers us to gain these treasures. In short, our desires become our gods. Lifetime mates, lovers, friends, achievements, monetary wealth, and material acquisitions all become more important than the One who created them all, and then the trouble begins. We watch these things teeter and fall from their pedestals. They are shattered before our very eyes, and we learn the painful lesson that what we have been holding dear is temporal at best.

It is important to note here that Ruth's mother-in-law, Naomi, and her husband had left Israel during a time of famine and headed to Moab, which was considered enemy territory, trying to find a way to maintain their way of life. It is ironic that, when Naomi returned to Israel, all the people she had left behind were still there and doing all right. They had weathered the storm and bounced back. They had stayed and trusted in God, and He had sustained them. Meanwhile, she lost everything. I do not condemn Naomi. I simply mean to raise the point that sometimes, when our personal empires are endangered, when our way of life drives us, we do not hear the direction of God. We are willing to do anything to secure our relationships, our holdings, our dreams. We decide we have to help God because, from where we stand, we can't see how He can fix things. We move out of season, out of time, and we lose more than we thought possible, all in the name of self-preservation. We move out from under the umbrella of God's protection, and we get wet. Wet with our own tears.

The confusing part of all this is that God will allow us to do as we like. To go where we want to go. He will even sustain us there for a time, but then He nudges us back to the center of His will by allowing the very things that carried us away to evaporate. Naomi eventually came around, going back to where she should have been in the first place. What a painful way to find God's will.

Of course, not every loss we experience comes because we made a wrong decision or failed to trust in God's provision. Sometimes our losses are just the natural order of living and dying, aging and seasonal changes. Even when we *do* hold things and those who are dear to us in balanced view, we must be cognizant of the fact that nothing lasts forever except our relationship with God. He does give us dear persons and prized possessions. It is His delight to do so, but never with the intention that they should become the center of our existence, our oxygen, or our lifeblood. Even when we give God His rightful place in our hearts, the cycle of life eventually leads us to the place of loss.

As the seasons change and summer gives way to winter, the most beautiful things die to make room for even fresher blooms in the coming season. The earth mourns their absence and then turns to welcome the new. We are bound to this earth in our minds, but our spirits forever stretch beyond to a place called eternity. And those things that are not spiritual can only last so long in this limited space of a place that we call earth and time. Man's measurement of God's infinite space. It is all we know. It is all that we can easily focus on. The here and now. But there is a bigger picture outside the expanse of our thoughts and beyond our comprehension. We must keep moving in order to reach that place. But first we must release what keeps us rooted to the spot where we stand. Celebrate and embrace what you have now, but don't cling too tightly. God will not be relegated to second place in our lives.

I think of the story told in 1 Samuel chapter 5 about the Philistines' god Dagon. The Philistines had stolen the Israelites' ark of the covenant—their representation of the presence of God—and stored it in Dagon's temple. The next morning the Philistines saw that the statue of Dagon had fallen on its face. They set it back up again, and the next day they found it had fallen off its pedestal once again. This time its head and hands had separated from its trunk. The Philistines' realization that they were dealing with something greater than their man-made god began to settle in.

Like the Philistines, we, too, try to set God up next to the things or people we treasure most and demand that He coexist peacefully wherever we place Him in our hearts. We lift our treasures up high and celebrate them while overlooking the Greater One. And then it happens. The people or the things that we've placed all our trust in make mistakes or fail us. They fall off their pedestals. And even so, we cling to them as our salvation and our source of joy and fulfillment, only to find in the end that they are completely incapable of filling the space in our lives we needed them to fill. I don't mean they are not good. I only mean they are not God. All good things eventually come to an end. The stock market rises and falls. Great positions are phased out. Jewelry and possessions are lost. People we love disappoint us, leave us, or die. Only One remains.

When something good in our lives comes to an end, I think we stand in shock thinking, *What will I do now?* The very foundation of our own identity can be shattered in many instances if we build our entire world around a person, thing, or dream. We are empty, shaken, beyond comfort, fearful of tomorrow. In the wake of my boyfriend's death, I found myself incapable of making decisions. My entire existence as I knew it had been rocked to its very foundation. I had planned on being married to and sharing decisions with this man for the rest of my life. What would I do now? He was no longer there to save me from the things I was afraid, or not sure enough about, to do on my own. And yet I had to move on. The first thing I had to do, and I believe the first thing Ruth had to do, was dismantle the idea that this man who had been the central theme of her life was the axis on which the universe turned. The world continued to turn. Instead of looking down, Ruth chose to look up and let go of her dependence on someone who could never have been all that she needed anyway. If your grief is over an event or the loss of something that was of great importance to you, the only way to retrieve a full life is to let go of what you are now clinging to.

For some, it is hard to conceive of the fact that something can be over when we feel we are where God put us in the first place. If nothing was wrong with our situation, why did it have to end? Simply because we have been called to something higher, because the season for where you were is now over, and because losses are inevitable. When Elijah fled Jezebel, God led him to a brook to drink and be refreshed. But eventually the brook dried up, and God told him it was time to move on to a new place of sustenance. If your source of love and nourishment has been depleted, rest assured that God has already arranged new provision for you. But you must be willing to stop clinging to the past and be open to the new possibilities. We cannot afford to cling too tightly to anyone or anything. The line between love and idolatry is a thin one.

So how do you know when someone or something is an idol in your life? When you believe you couldn't bear to live without it. We are all called to hold every facet of life loosely. I compare it to how we wear clothes. We all wear clothing, but we don't bind it to our bodies. (Well, some of us do! And find it uncomfortable.) For the most part, we allow it to hang and frame us. Yet with every movement we find it is still there. And so it is with everything in life. This analogy does not mean you are emotionally dead, unfeeling, and noncommittal. This just means you hold things in the right perspective. If the thing close to your heart is not an idol, then simply bow and say yes to God, who is not finished blessing you yet. Though, whenever you experience loss, the grieving process is real and necessary, paralysis is not. Idols are just that—idle. They can do nothing for us. Therefore it is fruitless to cling to them. Let go of the idols and instead cling to the One who is living and able to come to your aid.

➤ LOOKING INWARD ◄

- Where does God fit in with the desires of your heart?
- Do the objects of your affections circumvent your ability to keep them in the right perspective?
- Would the loss of these things or this person cause you to resign from living to your full potential? Why?
- Where might your expectations have become unrealistic? Be specific.
- Can you see any good coming out of your present loss? In what ways can this situation make you stronger?

➤ LOOKING UPWARD ◄

"What is more, I consider everything a loss compared to the surpassing greatness of knowing Christ Jesus my Lord, for whose sake I have lost all things. I consider them rubbish, that I may gain Christ" (Philippians 3:8).

GET OVER IT

Just as Ruth had to get on with the business of living where she was, Joseph also had to release what was behind him. But wouldn't you know it. About the time Joseph was all settled into being top dog in Egypt, his brothers, the ones who sold him into slavery, just had to show up. Truly all was well with Joseph. He was married and had two sons, the respect of everyone in Egypt, and the favor of the pharaoh. The famine hit just as Joseph predicted, but everyone was still thriving because of the plan he had laid out to store provision. And you guessed it: His brothers came to Egypt looking for food because there was none in Israel.

God has His own way of turning the tables at the appropriate time. Of putting the offender in the place of needing the offended. This is why living with a servant mentality is so important. In Scripture, in every instance where someone submits to serving another wholeheartedly, the outcome is the same: The servant is eventually exalted above the person served. The reverse is also true: Those who do their job grudgingly never rise to any level of note. Joshua and Caleb served Moses and held up his arms. They inherited his leadership when he died and led the people of Israel into the Promised Land. Elisha served Elijah and got the double anointing upon his departure. Jesus served mankind, washed the feet of the disciples, and is exalted above every other name in heaven and in the earth. Joseph first served his brothers as a young man and then served Potiphar as a slave, only to be promoted above them all.

Now here his brothers were at his door, looking for food. Joseph had the perfect opportunity to put them in their place and make them pay for all he had endured. But Joseph knew that if you do what is wrong, you will be paid back for the wrong you have done. God has no favorites who can get away with evil (Colossians 3:25). So Joseph proceeded wisely. He set appropriate boundaries to test the hearts of his brothers. He did not reveal who he was right away. Instead, he tested them and observed their behavior and attitudes—not out of spite, but to see if they could be trusted with his love again.

Maturity is a beautiful thing. The young boy who had once recklessly proclaimed his dreams and been hurt as a result was now a man who held his peace and considered more carefully who could be trusted with the valuable parts of himself.

This is a lesson that anyone who has been betrayed should learn and apply. Far too often we allow a wayward mate, an inconsiderate friend, or a dishonest associate back into our life without any thought of testing that person's intentions or character. We fail to set appropriate boundaries. If nothing has changed and the person is not willing to deal, in a healthy and honest matter, with what went wrong before, you are destined for a repeat of what already happened. Get counseling. Hash it out. Discuss what went wrong and what changes need to be made in order for the relationship to be restored. Set parameters for reestablishing trust. Make a new covenant you can both live with. If the other person is not willing to do these things, keep your distance until he or she is. This is basic wisdom for guarding your heart, and God holds you responsible to do just that.

So Joseph revealed his identity to his brothers only after testing them and taking note of the fact that they, too, had grown through the years. They were quick to repent, and he was quick to assure them that they had been forgiven. He did not nurse and rehearse the past with them. He did not rub the present in their faces. He did not try to make them feel bad about what they had done. (They felt bad enough.) Instead, Joseph did all he could to make them feel comfortable and accepted. Which I'm sure made them feel worse. Small wonder the Bible tells us not to repay anyone evil for evil. We are to "be careful to do what is right in the eyes of everybody. If it is possible, as far as it depends on you, live at peace with everyone.... 'If your enemy is hungry, feed him; if he is thirsty, give him something to drink. In doing this, you will heap burning coals on his head.' Do not be overcome by evil, but overcome evil with good" (Romans 12:17-18,20-21).

Well, that's contrary to what you said before, Michelle. How can I keep my distance and feed someone at the same time? By knowing your limits and what you can handle. By keeping wise *emotional* boundaries. By keeping a level attitude in your heart. Don't get excited and entrust too much too soon to those who haven't earned your trust. Be loving, but do not give access to the place where your tender spirit abides. Don't give your enemy ammunition to shoot you with. Keep what is valuable to you out of their reach. If your friends can't keep a secret, don't trust them with personal information. People instinctively know how far they can go with you. You control the signal.

Joseph was able to be the "better man" among his brothers because he got over the past. Over the betrayal. Over the pain of it all. He named his first son Manesseh, meaning, "God has caused me to forget all my troubles." Yes, it is possible for God to remove the sting of our past, but only if we allow Him to. Sometimes our pain becomes dear to us. We feel that it is our defense from being hurt again. But actually it perpetuates a vicious cycle. Superimposing our past over our future sabotages our present. It clouds the lessons we've learned that will make us better, wiser people.

Joseph chose to embrace the better life and let go of the old and terrible. He chose to get over it and get on with the business of living. What was done was done. Events of the past definitely had a bearing on where he was now, but "now" was a better place. That he was in a better place could not be overlooked. If God is able to tread our sins underfoot and hurl our iniquities into the depths of the sea, who was Joseph to go fishing in the lives of his brothers? Who was he to collect the dust? For what purpose? What good could come out of that? No, it would be far better for Joseph to keep moving forward.

For the sake of all concerned, mainly yourself, it is imperative to let go of whatever and whoever caused you pain. Get over it. Only then can you get on with it as well.

➤ LOOKING INWARD ◄

- What painful event constantly revisits your thoughts?
- Is the rehearsal of your pain keeping you from moving forward?
- How do you feel as you recall the incident?
- What prohibits you from letting go? Is it a worthy reason?
- Can you see any good emerging from your present struggle?

➤ LOOKING UPWARD ◄

"Shake off your dust; rise up, sit enthroned, O Jerusalem. Free yourself from the chains on your neck" (Isaiah 52:2).

LEARN YOUR LESSON

There is always a lesson. But we must search for it among the ruins. Like a diligent archaeologist, we must be determined to find the treasure. Joseph found his lesson and named his second child Ephraim in commemoration of it. Ephraim means "God has caused me to be fruitful in the land of my affliction." In answer to his brothers' plea for forgiveness, he soothed their wounded consciences by letting them know their ill intentions were merely a pawn in God's hand to get to the end result. He was quick to let them know what they had meant for evil had brought about the greater good. Wow! Joseph finally got it. The full impact and purpose of what he had been through.

Joseph's dream so long before of becoming a mighty leader wasn't just about him. It was part of an incredible plan. It was not about his personal gratification and achievement. It was about saving an entire nation. One man was saved to save one nation. That one nation was saved to save another nation. The tribe of Israel. What do you think Joseph would have done with that information if he had known all that at age thirteen? He would have been a self-centered mess—out of control! Or trying to make the plan unfold. Still, Joseph had to be prepared for the task at hand. When he first had the dream, he did not yet have the wisdom required for this very important mission. He had to be weaned from being a spoiled brat. Purged of pride. Fertilized with wisdom. Pruned to bear fruit. He yielded to all of it, no matter how it hurt.

No experience in Joseph's life was wasted. Not only did working in Potiphar's house equip him with administrative skills, but it also gave him the opportunity to learn the language, the customs, and the nature of the people he would one day be dealing with. He also learned what the common man in society felt. This knowledge would later help him gain the cooperation of the people as he served as overseer of the land. People like other people who have been where they are. Joseph was the grass-roots guy who made good. His gifts were celebrated and held in esteem. He walked in favor with God and man.

Also, being in the king's jail gave Joseph more administrative training and insight into Pharaoh, the man he would be dealing with later. I'm sure Joseph learned a lot about this leader's weaknesses, strengths, and sensitivities as he interacted with those who had been employed by him and were now in jail. I'm sure he learned what he should and should not do to maintain Pharaoh's favor.

Joseph could not have planned his training better himself. All these awful things were part of God's design to bring him into the awesome fullness of his destiny. As I've reflected over my own personal jolts, I have to admit I've always come out of them the better. Something good has come out of every despairing moment. I would have chosen another route to reach my victorious destination, but who is to say I would have reached it going my own way? This is where our finiteness has to bow to our sovereign and all-knowing God. We can trust that He truly knows best, even when His love allows us to be wounded.

If Joseph hadn't gone to prison, he would not have ended up in the palace. Let's look back for a moment and see this intricate design that no man would have chosen and yet God did. Was it God's preference for Joseph's way to be so hard? I think not, but He wove Joseph's weaknesses into the fabric of His design for this impetuous boy's life. His rite of passage to becoming a great man was the way of the cross. Dying to everything he held dear as he made the transition from the *pallet* he slept on to the *pit* he was sold from to *Potiphar's house* where he was falsely accused to the *prison* where he was seemingly forgotten to the *palace* where he was finally promoted. Five Ps. In Scripture, five is the number of grace. By God's grace, Joseph matured and learned his lessons well.

He learned that life was bigger than he was. That God's sovereign plan is all-encompassing. That God will use our mistakes and weaknesses to propel us toward our destiny and the fulfillment of His purposes. We cannot afford to have selfish dreams and self-involved desires. We were not made to function that way. No, the dreams and desires we harbor are planted in our spirits by God Himself. He knows what He wants to do with those dreams and desires. And He waits until we have released our own agendas. Which means they usually have to die first. He waits for us to bury them and walk away. Then He blows the dust off our crushed dreams and brings them to pass.

Nothing can be more rewarding in life than to weather a misfortune and to watch God transform it into a triumph. Not just for yourself, but for others. To look back and be able to acknowledge that the journey has been necessary is an important step toward your victory. In the end, you will be counted as a champion. So "endure hardship with us like a good soldier.... If anyone competes as an athlete, he does not receive the victor's crown unless he competes according to the rules" (2 Timothy 2:3,5). Unless he endures the training, plays fair, and learns his lessons well.

➤ LOOKING INWARD ◄

- What has your pain told you about yourself?
- Are your weaknesses clear to you? What are they?
- What lesson is emerging from your suffering?
- How can you equip yourself to welcome the truth?
- What can you find to celebrate in God's design as it unfolds in your own life?

➤ LOOKING UPWARD ◄

"He who gets wisdom loves his own soul; he who cherishes understanding prospers" (Proverbs 19:8).

WALK, DON'T RUN

How does one survive the grieving process? By taking it a day at a time. Step by step we inch toward wholeness. Two steps forward, three steps back. Then forward again until we begin to make true progress. Not every day will be a good day. That's all right. Good days will come, quietly, triumphantly, like the dawning of a new day. Weeping may endure for a night, but joy will come in the morning. It may not be tomorrow morning or the morning after that. But joy will meet you one morning. If you keep getting up.

Ruth and Naomi set off walking from Moab to Israel. For Naomi, the journey marked a return; for Ruth, a stepping out into the unknown. Both were going to where God wanted them. One step at a time. They did not reach Israel in a day. The journey took commitment, a constant forward movement. Wouldn't you love to be privy to the conversations they had along the way? Reflecting on days gone by. Speculating on their tomorrows. Making plans for what they would do when they reached their destination. I imagine they talked a lot and spent a lot of time thinking. I'm sure there were periods of time when they just walked silently, each lost in her own thoughts.

They collected their memories and tucked them into a safe place within their hearts. They stopped to rest when the heat of the day became too great for them to keep going, seeking shade until cool breezes blew across their path.

The grieving process is a delicate one. There is a time for nursing and rehearsing past events. A time when every memory and feeling has been vented and exhausted. A season of silence. Resting. Allowing God to mend the heart. There will be times when grief will overtake you. Bowing you over, causing you to stop until its wave has passed. Then there will be respites when cool breezes of comfort will blow. The urge to rush the process of healing must be resisted. As one who picks at a scab discovers, trying to find the new skin only creates an unwanted scar. We must let air and time do their work in our wounded hearts.

Just as Ruth and Naomi walked slowly, preserving their strength in order to reach their destination, we must walk patiently toward healing. Sorrow cannot be hurried. You can't leap ahead of it or hold it back once it decides its season is over. Grief is a friend that reluctantly bids you good-bye in its own time. Slowly extricating itself from your arms. Kissing you farewell once it feels you are strong enough to stand on your own. But it will walk with you for a while. Allow it. But don't count on it to remain.

Naomi, however, clung to her grief, and it turned into something else. Bitterness. It clouded her vision and made her way difficult. Don't go there. Don't become attached. Don't feel guilty about letting go. Don't blame others or things or God. Ruth released her grief as she walked, released it like a cape that had grown too heavy. Slowly, steadily, until she found an acceptance of her circumstances. She didn't blame life or adversity. She simply settled into the now and looked toward the future. What was on the horizon she didn't know. But she would find out one step at a time.

That's all any of us can do. Only One knows what is unknown to us. He has numbered our days, the good ones as well as the bad ones. He has spaced them out according to our ability to bear them. Therefore choose to trust and keep moving. Don't run. Don't become impatient with yourself.

Funny thing about morning: It comes whether you're ready for it or not. Its light overtakes the darkness and forces you to face the day. And so it is with life. The mortgage is still due. People expect you to function. Your boss expects you to produce. Life goes on...one day at a time. It has its way of pulling you back to the reality of the present.

Jesus said not to worry about tomorrow; today comes with enough troubles of its own. Do today well and deal with tomorrow...tomorrow. When manna rained upon the Israelites as they wandered in the wilderness, God told them to collect only what they needed for the day's food. Whenever they gathered more than they needed, it spoiled. Why? Because God was trying to teach them to depend on Him daily. "Give us this day our daily bread." A profound prayer. Fresh bread every day. Hot and nutritious. New every morning. Fresh grace to handle all that occurs within the space of twenty-four hours. No more. No less. So why do we struggle to reconcile massive blocks of time in our minds? It is unnecessary. It is also impossible. Deal only with what you are able to grasp for now. And that, my friend, would be today. You are only responsible for the moment you are in, minute by minute, step by step. God will be with you as you walk through your pain, wade slowly through your tears, and let suffering do its perfect work of mending in you. Whatever you do, don't run.

➤ LOOKING INWARD ◄

- Are you taking one day at a time or worrying about tomorrow?
- Are you trying to do too much too soon?
- What is within your power to do today?
- What small step can you take toward your healing today?

➤ LOOKING UPWARD ◄

"But those who hope in the LORD will renew their strength. They will soar on wings like eagles; they will run and not grow weary, they will walk and not be faint" (Isaiah 40:31).

FACE YOUR FEARS

After being hit by a car, as I mentioned earlier, I experienced great fear and apprehension when I had to walk across a street. As a matter of fact, at first I refused. I would get to the corner and stand there for a long time waiting for a moment when no cars were in sight. Of course this meant that I sometimes waited for a long time. Other pedestrians would come and go, and still I stood there, trying to calm the pounding of my heart. Many times I just hailed a cab. But my fear became expensive, and I realized I had to overcome my phobia. So I marched myself back to that fateful corner and purposely crossed it. And much to my fear's surprise, I made it across intact! Voilà! I was free! (I have to admit I got in the habit of making eye contact with any driver who might be waiting to turn at the corner.) But, bottom line, I was no longer a prisoner of my fear. And I could save some money getting where I had to go.

Learning your lesson doesn't mean you refuse to go where you've been before. That's not wisdom. That's fear. I'll never love again, trust again, do *that* again… All those "I'll nevers" (unless you're talking about drug use or some other dangerous habit) hinder us. They rob us of the freedom to live a full life. He who never risks anything will never gain anything worthwhile. God wants us to master our faith and extinguish our fears. In His mind, fear is a matter of personal choice. This is why Jesus said—in Michelle paraphrase—"Do not *allow* your hearts to be troubled. Trust in God. Trust in Me and My ability to help you. Fear not. I am going to give you a supernatural peace that the world at large will not be able to understand because they have not been able to grasp it. You won't be able to understand it yourself except to know that your confidence comes from

Me" (see John 14:27). *You mean my heart needs permission from me to be fearful, Michelle?* Yes, it does. We have the power to speak words of faith that turn our eyes away from our inability to cope and toward God's ability and willingness to give us the power we need to overcome.

Fear cannot remain in God's presence. He doesn't allow it. But I'm sure our recovering prophet Elijah couldn't believe his ears at first when God instructed him to go back the way that he had come. *You mean back to where that woman is waiting to kill me, Lord?! Back to that place that hurt me so deeply?* Yes, that would be the place He was talking about. Though sometimes God instructs us to leave a certain place, occasionally He tells us to go back. After we've passed through that place unscathed, however, we're going to continue on and carry out a new assignment. Elijah would face some different kings. Some other things that were greater than he was. "But don't worry," God told him, "I'm going to give you the help you need."

And God will do the same for you. He will never leave you or forsake you, my friend. And believe it or not, you are not the only one going through your specific trial. God told Elijah that seven thousand other prophets had not given in to the threat of their enemy. Just because Elijah couldn't see them didn't mean they didn't exist. He was not alone, just as you are not alone. Others have suffered and come through all right, even better for the experience! Well now, doesn't that just give you a faith boost? You are going to make it. You actually *will* be able to face some other obstacles bigger than yourself without fear. Not only that, but you won't have to face them alone. God will give you assistance: "I will not leave you comfortless: I will come to you" (John 14:18, KJV).

God instructed Elijah to train a new assistant, Elisha, to succeed him. Well, gee, doesn't a fellow get to nurse and rehearse his issues for a while before he has to pour his life into someone else? No, that is not how healing works. Our pain holds incredible lessons not just for us, but for others as well. Teach others what you are learning, and see how quickly your own scars heal. There is something about using your experiences for the sake of others. You begin to see the good in it for yourself. Ruth learned that when she reached out to Naomi. When you are responsible for someone other than yourself, you handle life differently. Someone expects the best from you. Rise to the occasion and be a fearless example. When you are protecting someone, there is no room for trepidation. The teacher cannot be weaker than the student.

Jesus went to the cross fearlessly. His only concern was being separated from His Father as He became sin for the world. That one thing He could not bear the thought of. But He dealt with it. He faced it dead on. He admitted His state in the Garden of Gethsemane. In Michelle paraphrase: "Father, if it is possible, let this cup pass from me. But if this is the only way to accomplish this mission, then so be it. I will endure the pain of being cut off from you because I know that the end of the matter will be greater than the beginning, and we will be together again" (see Matthew 26:39). When we have the assurance that in the end all will be well, we can catch sight of the joy on the other side of our fears and boldly go where we hesitated to go before.

Jesus firmly corrected Peter when this passionate disciple questioned the necessity of what He was about to go through. Jesus added that He would pray that Peter's fear would turn to faith so that he could turn and strengthen his brothers. Fear makes you useless to others as well as to yourself. It leaves you with a disappointing feeling of purposelessness. You become frozen in time, dying on the vine, because fear does not diminish your need to be who you are. Fear's effect is robbery of the highest degree. The part of you that wants to be free cries out for expression. Listen to that inner voice; follow its instructions. Embrace the truth that "God hath not given us the spirit of fear; but of power, and of love, and of a sound mind" (2 Timothy 1:7, KJV). This is God's gift to you: the power to love in spite of past experience. The power to possess a sound sense of God's protection and provision because you are aware of His promises. Anything contrary to His Word is a lie. Someone once said fear is faith turned inside out. False evidence appearing real. Only what God says is true. And that is the truth that will make you free—free to face your fears and conquer them.

➤ LOOKING INWARD ◄

- What is your greatest fear?
- What part of your fear is mere speculation?
- What do you know to be true about the situation you fear?
- What do you need to believe to get peace about this situation?
- What steps can you take to get past your fears?

➤ LOOKING UPWARD ◄

"Have I not commanded you? Be strong and courageous. Do not be terrified; do not be discouraged, for the LORD your God will be with you wherever you go" (Joshua 1:9).

BE OPEN

We are a resolute people. We make bold statements about what we will or will not allow to happen in our lives. We paint scenarios of how our careers, our lives, our relationships, our dreams should progress. When we're disappointed we quickly erect barriers to prevent repeat setbacks. We fail to be open. We unwittingly cut off all avenues to happiness and peace and wonder why it takes so long to reach them.

Yet timing is everything. There is a time for planting. A time for the seed to die in the earth before it can bear fruit. Ruth and Naomi arrived in Israel at harvest time. It was time for Ruth's harvest. She had suffered and endured. Little did she know she would glean food and a husband at the same time.

Ruth went into the fields to glean—that is, to pick up the grains left behind by the farmers for the poor. Her outward movements mirrored the inward. She also gathered the remains of her life in her thoughts. She went in order to survive. She and Naomi needed food to eat. But God had more than just survival in mind. As Ruth set her hand to do what she could do, God did the rest. He honored her commitment. In service to her mother-in-law, she would receive her reward.

While gleaning in the fields, Ruth unknowingly caught the eye of Boaz, a very wealthy relative on her husband's side of the family. As tradition had it in those days, the next of kin should redeem a widow in order to carry on the family name and keep all holdings in the family. To Naomi's knowledge that next of kin was Boaz. When Boaz showed an interest in Ruth's welfare and extended kindness to her, Naomi advised Ruth to let Boaz know she was in need of a redeemer. Ruth took her mother-in-law's advice.

The words of Boaz struck me as I read the conclusion to this story that started off with such misfortune. "'The LORD bless you, my daughter,' he replied. 'This kindness is greater than that which you showed earlier: You have not run after the younger men, whether rich or poor. And now, my daughter, don't be afraid. I will do for you all you ask. All my fellow townsmen know that you are a woman of noble character'" (Ruth 3:10-11). *Weelll!* Isn't that interesting? Boaz didn't expect a young woman like Ruth to consider an older man like him. Ruth probably hadn't thought she would end up with an older man either!

But Ruth was open. She had nothing to lose. She had already lost it all. *I'm open to new options.* I'm sure the words rang in her heart daily. *So... I have to go and glean in the fields behind the harvesters in order to have food? I never thought this is what my life would come to, but...I'm open. So Naomi thinks I should take the attention of Boaz seriously? He's not exactly what I had envisioned for a husband, but he is nice... Hey, I'm open!*

Because Ruth was open, she got more than she had ever dreamed. Boaz told her another redeemer was technically in line before him, but if that man was not willing to redeem Ruth, he would. He was willing to pay the bride price for her hand in marriage. And so, by the end of the day, the matter was settled. Ruth went on to marry wealthy Boaz and give birth to Obed, the grandfather of David, king of Israel.

And hopeless Naomi? She was not so hopeless anymore. Ruth and Boaz were married, and soon Naomi had a baby to love. The women surrounded her and proclaimed, "'Praise be to the LORD, who this day has not left you without a kinsman-redeemer. May he become famous throughout Israel! He will renew your life and sustain you in your old age. For your daughter-in-law, who loves you and who is better to you than seven sons, has given him birth.' Then Naomi took the child, laid him in her lap and cared for him. The women living there said, 'Naomi has a son'" (Ruth 4:14-17).

Naomi has a son. Wow! her arms that ached from emptiness were refilled. Talk about restoration. *God's* perfect restoration. Though Naomi and Ruth had different expectations for life, they each reaped far more because they remained open to God's direction. What if they had decided to lose themselves in mourning? They would have spent the rest of their days joyless and in poverty. What if Ruth had never allowed herself to love again, thinking in some way her grief would honor her dead husband? She would never have entered the lineage of Christ in such a profound way.

I find the Jewish tradition regarding so-called "kinsman redeemers" like Boaz to be providential. It forced a grieving wife not only to move on, but also to secure the heritage of her mate. As I mentioned, I believe we secure the heritage of loved ones by securing a life well lived in their honor.

Whenever the time comes for us to say good-bye to those we love, young or old, and they pass to the other side of eternity, we must remain open to new avenues of restoration and happiness. Whenever good dreams die, we must be willing to dream new ones and remain open to the idea that there are better dreams to dream.

We must remain open to God's personal plan for our lives and invite His personal touch on our lives. Yes, we must *ephphatha* ("be opened"). This was the word Jesus spoke to the deaf and dumb man in Mark 7:33-35. Jesus led him away from the crowd that had brought the man to Him, put His fingers into the man's ears, and then spit on His fingers and touched the man's tongue. The man became able to speak and hear plainly. On another day some people brought a blind man to Jesus and asked Him to heal his sight (Mark 8:22-26). Jesus led this man away from the village where they were, spit on his eyes, touched them twice, and restored his vision. Then Jesus told him not to return to the village, but to go home.

In order for these men to be healed, Jesus had to remove them from where they had been. Then He touched them. Deeply. Personally. I don't think that anyone standing in a healing line expects to be spit on! But Jesus knew they needed more than a touch. They needed something more personal from God. When two people kiss each other deeply, they exchange something of themselves with each other. Jesus imparted something from within His very being to these men.

The once-blind man was instructed not to go back to the village. Not to return to where he had been. He was not to surround himself with the people he had grown dependent on before. He was not to revisit the views and opinions he had held before. It was time to do away with codependency and victim mentality. We, too, need to be removed from old trains of thought, habits, places, people, anything that keeps us in the same old frame of mind.

Seeing, hearing, speaking. Three important areas affected by a personal touch from God. Pain affects how we see things, how we interpret what we hear, and how we express ourselves. What we see and what we hear affects what we say. What we say affects what we become. Therefore, Jesus deals with every aspect of our inner person. God wants us to be whole, to be delivered from all that hinders us from functioning as we should. He is willing and longing to give us a personal touch. But we must be open to it.

I found the reverse fairy tale *Shrek* rather refreshing. An ogre rescues a beautiful princess, Fiona, from a fortress guarded by a dragon. She has been expecting a handsome prince. Quite to her surprise she finds herself falling in love with the ugly ogre. The ogre is filled with pain as he realizes he is falling for the princess. Trying to shield himself from the rejection he is sure to experience, Shrek rejects Fiona before she can reject him. Little does he know she is under a curse. She is a beautiful princess by day, an ugly ogre by night. The curse will be broken by a kiss from her one true love. Finally the truth comes out, and they admit their love for each other. They kiss, and an incredible thing happens. She is turned into an ugly ogre permanently! In dismay she says, "But I don't understand! I was supposed to be beautiful." To which Shrek replies, "You are beautiful to me." Off they go to live happily ever after. Truly beauty is in the eye of the beholder.

Life rarely turns out as we expect it to. But the important thing is that it turns out for the good. We seldom find happiness where we look for it, but we often find ourselves surprised by joy in the least expected places.

So a loved one has gone on? Be open. A dream has been destroyed? A longing disappointed? Be open. You've received unexpected bad news? Be open. Be open to a personal touch from God. An occasion for Him to glorify Himself as He acts on your behalf. To bring you not only restoration, but newness of life above and beyond your expectations.

➤ LOOKING INWARD ◄

- Describe how you have decided your future should go.
- Which doors have you closed in your life? in your heart?
- Do changes scare you? Why?
- What new beginning would you select for yourself?
- Are you open to God's creativity at this time? Explain.

➤ LOOKING UPWARD ◄

"Let the morning bring me word of your unfailing love, for I have put my trust in you. Show me the way I should go, for to you I lift up my soul" (Psalm 143:8).

DO WHAT YOU'VE
NEVER DONE BEFORE

They say if you want something different to happen in your world, you have to do something different. I love the book *Who Moved My Cheese?* It's the story of some mice who found a block of cheese and just assumed they could feed off it forever. But one day they discovered that the cheese was gone. Oh my! This presented quite a problem for the group of stick-in-the-muds. They refused to accept the fact that the cheese was gone and resolved to wait for it to magically reappear or be replaced. They kept visiting the same spot day after day to no avail. The other set of mice took off through the maze of life in search of new cheese, and eventually they found it.

Many of us are like those mice who won't move on to a new location. Or we assume our mate will always be there. The money will always be there. Our health will always be good. Our children will always behave. Our personal world will remain unchanged. We assume that we can stand in the same spot and that one day all the things that we don't like will miraculously change for the better with no effort on our part. Instead, one day, we find to our dismay that our assumption was wrong. We are still standing in the same spot, but everything around us has shifted to a place we don't like. In our shock, anger, and disappointment, we dig in our heels and demand that everything return to normal. But it doesn't. We stand defiantly and wonder how everyone around us could have the audacity to get on with living while we are dying right before their eyes. Of course, we don't have to. We, too, can move on and try out a new path. And yet we can't quite seem to dislodge ourselves from the way things used to be. We choose to remain rooted in memories of the way we were.

Do we hate change or what? What is it about us? Why do we become mortified when we realize that life around us is constantly changing? Oh, the energy God must expend urging us to get on with the business of living life! We keep stopping and parking. Stopping and parking. And then we wonder why nothing happens. We've been standing in the same spot, that's why. Life has moved on. We must move with it. It is important to remember that one particular event in our life is not our destination. Life is a journey. The scenery and characters are always changing.

The comfort in all this is that, even when everything is changing, God does not change. He is as faithful as He ever was. As compassionate. As protective. As concerned as ever about solidifying your welfare. Yet He says that He will do a new thing. Well, which one is it? Is He staying the same or doing a new thing? The answer is both. He is the same, and He is always creating. Creating a new future that accommodates all the twists and turns of your life. He is not shocked when your mate leaves. He is not dismayed by your sudden financial demise. He is not appalled by the rebellion of your children. He is not thrown by your bad health report. He is not paralyzed by the death of your dear one. He has already leaped ahead to the solution, to preparing a way for you to overcome all that happens along your life journey.

But you must cooperate. When He says let go, you must fling your hands to the wind and let Him take your burden. When He beckons you to proceed, to turn left or right, you must be willing to follow, no matter where He leads you. I throw in this caveat because you can bet He will not lead you through a rehashed situation. He will take you down a brand-new path.

Think about this: Ruth decided to go to Israel—a foreign country hostile toward her people—with Naomi. I doubt Ruth had ever left Moab before, but she was leaving now. Instinctively she knew there would be no new life for her in this place. It was time to take a risk. Wipe the slate. Get rid of the list of how life should have been in order to see what it would become. Scary stuff. But necessary. Remember, you can't move forward and look back at the same time. You'll either have a collision or trip over your own feet. In either case, you are in for quite a spill.

The first thing I did after my boyfriend died was move to a new apartment. We had been living together—at the time I was not a Christian—and I knew that, if I stayed, I would never get past my grief. The place held too many reminders of him, too many things to keep me entrenched in my pain. The next thing I did was get busy. I dove into my work with a vengeance. I found new activities to be involved in, activities I had before never thought I'd enjoy, but they became my lifeline as I met new people and developed new interests. The pain subsided as I found new life outside my internal space. Eventually, as I mentioned before, the events surrounding his death and my need to move on propelled me into the arms of the One who would never leave me, no matter my circumstances.

So "forget the former things; do not dwell on the past" (Isaiah 43:18). Out with the old, in with new beginnings. It has been said you cannot continue to do the same thing and expect different results. You can no longer ignore the end that your actions continually invite. What should you do differently next time? For some who are experiencing repeat failures in a relationship or dream, it is time to deal with yourself. Ask what the repeat factor has been in your mind-set. In the other person involved. In the situation. Nothing new will happen if you insist on your old attitude.

Perhaps this is the rationale of big corporations that get rid of loyal workers just before implementing new measures. The general way of thinking is that older employees will resist new measures. Or as Jesus said, "You can't put new wine in old wine skins. The old skin will burst. But if you put new wine in new wineskins they will both be preserved" (see Matthew 9:17). The person who says, "Why can't we just keep doing it the way we've always done it?" spreads dissension and creates difficulty. Disgruntled employees take time to sort out, and time is money. So to sidestep lost production time, management brings in new employees with no recall of the past. It seems cruel, but the rationale is based on tried and true experiences.

You see, old wineskins shrink and get hard. When new wine is poured into them, they can't expand. The hard skins crack and burst, and the wine is lost. But new wineskins are soft and pliable. When new wine is poured into them, they take on the shape of the liquid that has been poured inside. They adapt to the shape of what is inside as it settles in. We, too, settle into a way of life, take the shape of what is already in our world. When the shape of our world changes, we find ourselves set in our ways, unable to flex our horizons and accommodate something new. We explode. We are shattered when forced to take on something new. This renders us useless.

With the help of God, we can be flexible. Roll with the punches. Welcome the possibilities that each new trial presents us. Our ability to be flexible will determine whether we become the master or the mastered. If life is truly a journey, we must be willing to move on in search of a new life and better experiences, knowing our present circumstance does not speak to the end of the matter. After all, God, who has begun a good work in us, is able to carry it on to completion (see Philippians 1:6).

We must partner with God in this endeavor. If we refuse, He will wait until we are willing to move. If we don't do what we need to do, God will do it for us by allowing the circumstances of our life to force our hand. That is usually not a pleasant experience. Believe me, time has a way of bringing us to conclusions we could have drawn earlier. When we've finally had enough of the same old thing, doing something different begins to look awfully good. But why wait until then?

Ruth did not allow her life to stagnate. When her grief abated, she got ready to move on. Do something different. Change the scenery of her life. Break free of the things that bound her to her old existence. Step out in faith anticipating something better. Even if she couldn't see the future with her eyes, she trusted in her heart that this God her mother-in-law believed in would have mercy on her and make a way for her. And on that note she dared to embrace the unknown and do something she had never done before.

➤ LOOKING INWARD ◄

- What parts of your past are you clinging to?
- What scares you about doing something new?
- What choices are before you now?
- What is something that you've always longed to do but never done? Could this be the time to do it?
- What is holding you back from embarking on a new adventure?

➤ LOOKING UPWARD ◄

"And no one pours new wine into old wineskins. If he does, the wine will burst the skins, and both the wine and the wineskins will be ruined. No, he pours new wine into new wineskins" (Mark 2:22).

RELEASE THE UNKNOWN

"The unknown." Those words send tremors up our spine. How can you control what you cannot see, grasp, or anticipate? I happen to be one of those people who can't stand the suspense. When the plot thickens in a story I'm reading and the hero falls into certain danger, I flip to the end to make sure he's going to be all right before I continue. I just can't endure the drama in peace if I don't know the ending. Most of us are like that about *life!*

So when God says, "I know the plans I have for you, plans to prosper you and not to harm you, plans to give you hope and a future"—or, as the King James translation says, "thoughts of peace, and not of evil, to give you an expected end" (Jeremiah 29:11)—we scream, "Well, could You just let me in on those plans!" Ah, but alas and alack, He doesn't. What can we do at a time like this to make ourselves more comfortable? Release ourselves to the unknown without forsaking our desire.

Well, that sounds good in theory, but how does one do that? Let's face it, what else can we do? If we take stabs in the dark, we will only get in our own way and ultimately hurt ourselves. Simply trusting God—though the meter on that will move up and down on any given day—is far simpler. A wonderful song encourages, "When you can't see God's hand, trust His heart." If you really believe that God loves you and wants the best for you, you must believe that everything is working toward the greater good in your situation. Because it all does, pure and simple.

Consider someone like the mother who lost her child because of a drunk driver. She transformed her pain into positive energy and formed the organization Mothers Against Drunk Driving (MADD), becoming a force to provoke awareness and change that now benefit many. And what about the man who created Post-Its by accident. To his horror, he discovered the sticky solution he had applied to the back of note-sized pieces of paper did not stick permanently as it was supposed to. Today people around the world slap temporary reminders on every smooth surface and are happy that the glue didn't work. One man's mistake, in his eyes a failed mission, became beneficial to the masses.

The truth of the matter is that "the unknown" is the big picture I keep referring to. Too often we are too busy gazing at the one troublesome spot in our lives. We fail to comprehend the magnitude of our existence, to understand that our life is *not just about us.* It is about us *all* as a whole. Our pain births something in us that affects others. Or at least it should. Some pain cannot be avoided, but all pain should be used for the greater good.

Jesus understood that His death was not just about Him. Nor was it just about the people who didn't understand or like Him. It was about the salvation of the world. Moses' accidental killing of an Egyptian drove him to the backside of the desert, where he discovered his true calling as a mighty leader born to lead the children of Israel out of bondage.

"The unknown" jolts us out of our comfort zone and forces us to see beyond ourselves and our immediate dreams—if we choose to look. Closing our eyes is not a healthy choice. It will do no one any good if we fold deeper inward, become paralyzed, and miss the opportunities for joy and fulfillment that await us. Consider Ruth, who bravely made the choice to pursue a future she couldn't be sure of in a place that was hostile to her people. Still, she took the risk. She gained another chance for love and won the prize for her leap of faith.

If you insist upon knowing everything that is going on, if you are an admitted "control freak," you will stunt your progress. Opening your hands and releasing what you cannot control leaves you open to grasp what you can. So purpose to focus on the immediate. What can you do today to improve the quality of your life, although it is not exactly as you like it? What can you do to improve others' lives? Start small. Touch someone close to you. Listen to someone else's problem. Pick up one shattered piece at a time. Be open to friendship, even though you long for romance. Take one day at a time. Speak one word at a time, even though you feel volumes churning in your soul.

I recall dissolving into tears once when I accidentally wiped out an entire chapter I had written on my computer. A friend would not bend to my hysteria, but calmly said, "Well, this time you will write it better than before." And so I began again. You know what? He was right.

When confronted with the death of Lazarus, Jesus said He was glad for the sake of those who were living because now God would be glorified. How? He knew that with the passing away of Lazarus something more powerful than Lazarus was about to be resurrected—faith in God for all concerned. Until then all that He had shared with them was just theory, but now it would become something better. It would become reality. Remember, you don't need a miracle until you need a miracle. God delights in showing up in the hard places and making something wonderful out of the terrible. But that doesn't happen until we release the unknown and embrace His ability to work out the details we cannot fathom, fix, or even anticipate.

Oh, the stories I could tell of survivors in my own life! One woman I know was a happily married housewife with a successful husband. She lost him to cancer and found herself bankrupt shortly thereafter. Two nervous breakdowns later she picked herself up and went into survival mode for the sake of her young daughter, who had been born with physical disabilities. After writing a song on a whim with a couple of colleagues, she stumbled into the career of being a Grammy award–winning songwriter.

When this woman's husband died, she "didn't know" what she was going to do. She "didn't know" how she would survive. But God knew. Being squeezed out of her comfort zone into the unknown led her to become not only a successful songwriter but an incredible minister. Today her messages set countless people free. She released the unknown and did what she could do. That's all any of us can do.

➤ Looking Inward ◄

- What is it about the unknown that worries you most?
- What steps can you take to trust God for your future?
- In what ways has God turned your past tragedies or mistakes into something positive that you could not see at the time?
- In what ways can you begin to use your pain to improve someone else's life?
- Are you a candidate for a miracle?

➤ Looking Upward ◄

"A man's steps are directed by the LORD. How then can anyone understand his own way?" (Proverbs 20:24).

WHEN LIFE HITS HOME

They were established. Had prime real estate holdings. Were pillars of their community, noted and respected. Business was going well, increasing in profit daily, and they were sampling all the rewards. Their calendar was full of social events, and they were in regular attendance at all the most important functions, including those at the temple. The future seemed rosy and secure. Then, suddenly, they found themselves conquered, evicted from their homes, stripped of everything precious they owned, and transported to a hostile environment where no one knew who they were. Their illustrious reputation and stellar family lineage got lost in the shuffle of a busy foreign society. No one returned their calls. They were little fish in a massive pond. They got no respect. As a matter of fact, they were looked down on, considered unqualified for prime employment positions. All of a sudden they were forced to live in neighborhoods they would never have considered and work jobs they hated even more. This had to be a bad dream! A big mistake!

You've found their story laced throughout this book. The people I'm talking about are the Israelites who found themselves in captivity in Babylon. It was a bad scene. Though they didn't like where they found themselves, they had to play it out. But their story could well be ours at any given point in our lives.

We've all seen the drama played out in the lives of others around us, but few of us imagine ourselves starring in the central plot of life, when everything around us escapes our control. We all experience captivity, the awful feeling of helplessness to master a situation in our lives. But you know a good story isn't a good story unless it develops unexpected twists and turns that keep us on the edge of our seats. It's called creating momentum. Whether it is anxiety or hope that keeps us put, anticipating the outcome, we determine to see the story through to the bitter end. We've got to find out what will happen!

Recently on a plane ride, most of the passengers and I watched an action movie. Right before the end, after the hero had just delivered a cliff-hanger line, the tape was interrupted and the movie stopped. Well, the plane was up for grabs. People got up. They murmured. People were disturbed. They did not appreciate being left hanging. The flight attendant announced that the video equipment was out of her control. She could not rewind to where we had left off. However, the movie would begin again and play in its entirety. We would have to watch the entire movie again in order to find out the end. Two hours later I looked around that plane and everyone including myself had flipped between the various channels but returned to find out the conclusion of the movie.

The situation reminded me of life. Unfortunately, we can't push a fast-forward button to peek ahead at our tomorrows. Neither can we rewind our lives to revisit or erase the defining moment that led us to where we presently are. But one thing is certain: A Master has written the script of our life's story. He is a consummate director, and He knows the end of the story. The bottom line for me on any good movie is that it has happy ending. The hero fights the good fight and wins the heroine, carrying her off to happier tomorrows. We are guaranteed that very same end.

Jesus said, "In my Father's house are many rooms; if it were not so, I would have told you. I am going there to prepare a place for you. And if I go and prepare a place for you, I will come back and take you to be with me that you also may be where I am" (John 14:2,3). Though the troubles of this present life seem unbearable, God promises that hope and eternal joy await us. In the meantime we must determine not to leave our seats. We must press toward the finish and read the credits.

Life: The Movie. Written by God. Produced by the Holy Spirit. Directed by Jesus Christ. Starring you as The Overcomer. And you don't star alone. You have been surrounded by a tremendous supporting cast. Consider those troubled Israelites who eventually learned to thrive where they were, even occupying great stations of influence in the place of their initial captivity. Consider Elijah, Job, Joseph, Ruth, Abigail, and a host of others who struggled as you and I do with their personal circumstances. They, too, stood dismayed as the troubles hit home for them personally. And though we only have one account of their struggles, I am sure they had more. Such is the cycle of life. However, based on what they learned from the first act, they apparently did not have predictable repeat performances.

You don't have to either. Live and learn. As long as the world turns we must be prepared for the continuing saga of this thing called life, all the disappointments, as well as the joys. After all, the choice is yours. Hit the pause button if you must, but don't hit stop. Take a deep breath and realize you do have some say in the script of your unfolding drama. The lines are written, but you can ad-lib, be creative, anticipate the next line, and be ready with a comeback. Remember, no guts, no glory.

PART VI

GETTING ON WITH IT

M y t h
Life is tough and then you die.

➤ ➤ ➤

T r u t h
You have made known to me the path of life; you will fill me with joy in your presence, with eternal pleasures at your right hand.

PSALM 16:11

RELEASE

YOUR CAPTORS

Though our brave widow Ruth settled into Israel without much apparent difficulty, the Israelites who were captured and taken to Babylon had a few more struggles when they had to settle in enemy territory. As if that wasn't bad enough, it seemed that God wasn't giving them any breaks.

Just when you think God couldn't ask you to do something more difficult than settle into a situation you may not like, He goes to another level. "Seek the peace and prosperity of those who cause you difficulty" (see Jeremiah 29:7). Whoa! Now that is tough! *I don't want my enemies to be blessed, Lord. I want them to choke on something horrible and die a slow and painful death. I want them to feel the pain I have experienced because of their actions.* We can all relate to feeling this way, but the irony of it all is that if you were to have your wish, the experience would be lost on your enemies. They wouldn't even get the point that they were suffering because of what they did to you. They would be too busy finding someone else to blame, and the cycle of pain would continue in an ever-growing circle of vengeance and mayhem. Let it go. Bless your enemies. Do not curse them.

Why bless and forgive? So that God can continue to forgive and bless you. "If you do not forgive men for the things they do to you, your Father will not forgive your sins" (see Matthew 6:15). He will not do for you what you are not willing to do for others. So forgive from the heart those who hurt you. This might be difficult at first. Ask God to help you press past the offense. If you truly do this, you will be able to bless your enemies without flinching. Bless them and not look for something terrible to befall them. Keep at it. Bless them until you mean it, really mean that you want God to perform good in their lives. Then you will receive the same blessing that you give.

In every instance recorded in Scripture, when someone despised others, cursed them, or was consumed in jealousy, God would bless the person who was the object of those bad feelings all the more. Why? Because He is a defender of the defenseless. Because He watches the backs of those who walk unaware of the arrows that fly by day and night. Because He will remind us that He is the one in charge. He will bless whom He pleases, regardless of our opinion of them. We must first do things His way, which will free Him to carry out what He determines to be just. Don't make God have to stop and fix you before He can deal with the situation and your offender.

So that husband who left you for a "better" model…that employer who ignored your seniority, promoted the junior employee, and let you go instead…that abusive parent who has never had a good word to say to you…that injustice in the form of person or circumstance that has you stinging right now…let it go. Pray for those who use you, abuse you, lie to you, betray you. Whatever they have done or continue to do, let it go!

Whether extreme or minute, retaliation never works to the benefit of those who seek revenge. A man walks into his old office and shoots everyone in sight. Does he feel better? No. And on top of that, now he's in big trouble. Before his problem was only unemployment. That could have been rectified. But *this*…there will be no fixing *this*. This is a mess that will have lasting repercussions. *But, Michelle, I'd never hurt anyone!* Perhaps you are merely bad-mouthing someone who offended you. That kind of behavior only puts you in a bad light while the other person moves on.

Why should you bless whoever has messed up your plans for a hassle-free life, whoever is giving you grief because he or she seems to have power over you? The answer is simple according to God: Because if they have peace and prosper, so will you (see Jeremiah 29:7). When a tyrant is distracted by good things, his grip loosens.

There is no need for revenge, repayment, or even the final word. "Do not take revenge, my friends, but leave room for God's wrath, for it is written: "It is mine to avenge; I will repay,' says the Lord" (Romans 12:19). But here is how that repayment works: The Lord will replace whatever was stolen from you. Repayment will most likely not come from the one who took what was dear to you. Chances are, that person would never be able to do anything to make you feel better anyway.

Consider the family of a loved one whose murderer receives the death penalty. Does it replace the pain from the death of their departed? No. Justice has been done, but their loss has not been restored. And what about dealing with offenders who continue to do wrong and seem to get away with it? If they keep on doing what they are doing, their deeds will catch up with them without your help: "In due time their foot will slip; their day of disaster is near and their doom rushes upon them" (Deuteronomy 32:35).

So release your offenders. Pray for them. Free yourself to receive something better. As Jesus hung on the cross, considering Judas who had betrayed Him, the disciples who had abandoned Him, the Pharisees who had lied about Him, the fickle crowd that had used Him and then turned on Him, He had one thing to say about them all: "Father, forgive them, for they do not know what they are doing" (Luke 23:34). *Next!* His mind was already on the bigger picture, on where He was going and what His death and resurrection would accomplish.

Similarly, your willingness to "die" to how you think things should go in your life will accomplish something as well. It will free God's hand to give you pleasant surprises. So don't get distracted. Stay focused on being spiritually and emotionally whole, no matter how fragmented you might feel because of what has occurred in your life.

Blessing those who have hurt you will free you to get back on course.

Do not allow yourself to be bound to the offense. In some cases we cannot escape the presence of those who have caused us suffering. We are stuck with them. What is one to do? Bless them. Convict them with kindness. Let your graciousness do the work that no horrible attitude could. Melt a heart of stone. Cause wayward souls to see their error. And if not, then surely God will deal with them when judging their attitude—as He will deal with you and yours.

Consider these words of Jesus:

> But I tell you, Do not resist an evil person. If someone strikes you on the right cheek, turn to him the other also. And if someone wants to sue you and take your tunic, let him have your cloak as well. If someone forces you to go one mile, go with him two miles. Give to the one who asks you, and do not turn away from the one who wants to borrow from you.
>
> You have heard that it was said, "Love your neighbor and hate your enemy." But I tell you: Love your enemies and pray for those who persecute you, that you may be sons of your Father in heaven. (Matthew 5:39-45)

What is He saying? Does He want us to be doormats? Absolutely not! He is giving us the key to possessing secret power. He was saying give them another chance but not from the same vantage point. Take the upper hand! So much of what offends us has to do with the principle of the matter, that is, what we think others *should* or *shouldn't* have done to us. Blessing them, however, going the extra mile on their behalf when we think they don't deserve it, gives us power and freedom. How empowering it is when you act of your own will and not out of obligation or coercion! That extra mile places your oppressor in your debt. It puts you back in the driver's seat. *You* chose to go the extra mile. *You* chose to give above and beyond what had been asked of you. No one made you do it. *You* chose to do it! How liberating! Exercising the power of choice is a major coup on your part. What you choose to give you can pick back up again. But if someone takes it from you, it's no longer yours to claim.

Jesus said He chose to lay down His life. *He* chose. Not Herod. Not Pilate. Not the traitorous crowd. It was *His* choice. "No one takes it from me, but I lay it down of my own accord. I have authority to lay it down and authority to take it up again. This command I received from my Father" (John 10:18). There it is.

If someone offends you, don't go tit for tat. Don't return the offense, the pain, the hurtful words. Don't withdraw either. BUT change your position. Allow the person access to the other cheek. BUT set boundaries. Don't flee from the person. Take a stand. BUT approach your dealings differently. Do not allow what you allowed before. Restructure your interaction to open the door to a healthier exchange. Disallow continued offensive behavior. Jesus was not suggesting you volunteer for pain. He was merely saying, "Don't stoop to the level of the one who delivers disappointment. Be open to the concept of change. Have a different strategy. Be wise as a serpent but gentle as a dove" (see Matthew 10:16). Don't allow others to direct the flow of your emotions.

I will say it again: The only person you can control is yourself. The only person you can *change* is yourself, so why not change for the better? Be a person who doesn't respond to pain in such a way that you change for the worse. Instead, bless your offenders through prayer. Bless them with kindnesses. Bless them by doing something for them that they never asked you to do. Bless; do not curse. Forgive; do not embrace hatred. Release; do not bind yourself to offenses. Let God repay what has been stolen. You focus on moving forward.

➤ LOOKING INWARD ◄

- Whom are you blaming for your situation? Who has the power in it?
- What would you like to see happen to that person?

- Is God's goodness reliant on anyone's actions? Why or why not?
- What or whom do you need to release in order to move forward?
- Can you pray for that person now? What is an "extra thing" you can do for him or her?

➤ LOOKING UPWARD ◄
"But I tell you: Love your enemies and pray for those who persecute you, that you may be sons of your Father in heaven" (Matthew 5:44).

4 3

DON'T JUST BLOOM!
FLOURISH!

God can give the weirdest advice at the strangest times. Consider this
example: "Plant gardens, and eat the fruit of them" (Jeremiah 29:28, KJV).
As if the Israelites weren't disheartened enough by their captivity, they
would have to provide their own sustenance too. Uh-huh. Not only will
you reap what you sow in your suffering, but you will also eat it. So check
your seeds.

Why plant? Why invest anything in a place where you don't want to
be? in the life of someone who seems undeserving? Why plant in a place
that looks as if everything around you—resources, relationships, promising opportunities—has dried up? Well, because we don't know everything.
Things can change overnight. Or they may stay the same but lead to a
better-than-expected end, as they did for Ruth.

But more important, it is God's premier desire that we always bear
fruit, no matter what. When God created man, He put him in a garden
"to work it and take care of it" (Genesis 2:15). Every living thing He created has reproductive power to produce more of the same, to replenish the
earth with good things. Every animal, every flower, every tree has the ability to reproduce itself from a seed.

What type of fruit are we supposed to produce? First things first: the
fruit of the Spirit! Love, joy, peace, patience, kindness, goodness, faithfulness, gentleness, and self-control (Galatians 5:22-23). These special crops
usually become more lush when fertilized by trials and tests. God uses
such circumstances to saturate our hearts and wash away the grime of the
world so that true beauty within us can be revealed. How do we get that

type of fruit to grow in us? By letting our roots grow down into God. Then we can draw up nourishment from Him and grow in faith, strong and vigorous in the truth we were taught (Colossians 2:7). The truth of His Word incubates attractive fruit!

Ever strolled past the fruit counter and seen a delicious red apple, all washed and waxed, sitting there? Immediately your mouth begins to water. You won't be satisfied until you hold one in your hand and take a big bite. The explosion of clean, fresh flavor will refresh you, and you long for it. So it is with the people we know who possess the aforementioned fruits: These people refresh our spirit. We love being around them. We seek them out in times of trouble or in times of peace because of what they offer us. This is the same fruit that attracts people to the kingdom of God initially. Through the Spirit's fruit in our lives, they get to taste and see that God is good!

What happens when we are not fruitful? We repel others and displease God. Gaining His displeasure garners His disregard. Think about it. If you planted a garden and all the plants but one produced amazing blossoms, what would you do with that dry and tired one? You would probably dig it up, throw it away, and plant a new one. After all, it doesn't produce what you want from it. It detracts from the beauty of the garden. Visitors say the same thing when they notice that one nonproducing plant: "Ooh, what happened there?" Well, that just wouldn't do, would it?

That's the way Jesus felt about the fig tree He encountered on the road to Jerusalem (see Matthew 21:18-19). He was hungry and its leaves were in full bloom, so He went to see if there were any figs on the tree. He discovered no fruit, only foliage (it wasn't fig season), so He cursed the tree and said, "May no one ever eat fruit from you again." I can just imagine your reaction. *Why would He do a thing like that! How cruel! It wasn't the poor fig tree's fault; it wasn't fig season!* This is true. However, the tree shouldn't have been masquerading as if it were in full bloom. Jesus saw something wrong with this tree at its root. When the fruit did come, something would be wrong with it, and it could make someone sick. Jesus cursed it so that no one else would be negatively affected by what the tree offered.

A lot of people are like that fig tree. They look real good until you get up close, until someone requires or needs something from them. That's when you discover the real deal: There's no fruit there, only pretty foliage. Perhaps the parasites of bitterness, selfishness, and faithlessness fed on the good seed that was originally planted in their hearts and scarred it, affecting their ability to produce anything good to offer others. They are suspicious in nature, unwilling to yield anything to anyone. They are unable to discern the seasons of their lives and don't understand when to give and when to withhold. They have decided they will never again be taken advantage of, and they stop bearing fruit. Those who get too close will quickly learn that they may look good, but they have nothing life-giving to offer. This disappoints God because they are rejecting the purpose for their existence.

For those of you who just had a full-blown panic attack asking, "Will God throw me away? Will Jesus curse me?" the answer is absolutely not. God isn't willing to allow anyone to perish and exhibits great patience because of Jesus' intercession on our behalf. A great illustration of this is found in another story of a fig tree, recorded in Luke 13:6-9. A man who planted a fig tree checked it time and time again to see if there was any fruit on it. After three years, he finally got tired of it and told the gardener to cut it down, but the gardener asked that he give it one more chance. He promised to give it special attention and plenty of fertilizer. That is what the Lord does for us. He carefully nourishes us to fruitfulness.

Jesus said, "You did not choose me, but I chose you and appointed you to go and bear fruit—fruit that will last. *Then* the Father will give you whatever you ask in my name" (John 15:16, emphasis added). Interesting connection, isn't it? When we bear fruit, we get the Father's attention and favor. And when we don't, what can we expect? Not much. Only what we are able to produce in our own strength. That can get exhausting. It is in times like those that Jesus offers us His assistance. I suggest you take it.

Your fruit affects your reputation. And God's. When you produce good fruit, others are willing to help you because God goes before you with His favor. Become known for anything opposite of what the fruit of the Spirit is all about, however, and people won't like you. No one likes a harsh, hateful, impatient person. Where does that leave you? You are stuck—not a victim but a volunteer—because you've *chosen* to go through life the hard way, striving in your own flesh rather than walking in the Spirit.

Your fruit also includes the work of your hands. Good fruit is excellence in the marketplace. As I mentioned in chapter 20, excellence opens the door for you to prosper. God cannot and will not bless a mess. He is a God of excellence.

Remember, your fruit is what will sustain you as you wait for your situation to change. It is what you will eat. "A cheerful heart is good medicine, but a crushed spirit dries up the bones" (Proverbs 17:22). Nurture your spirit by choosing joy and trusting in God daily. This is up to you. Oh yes, it is! Unless your depression is physiological in nature, the choice is yours. If our depression is born out of what you think, take control of your thought life. Depression is hard work and a bitter stew. Choose an easier occupation and a more tasty dish. As you choose a good attitude daily, your action will soon become a habit. The result will do wonders for your mental health and physical strength, and you will begin to positively affect others around you. Their response to you will change, and your way will become easier. "Pleasant words are a honeycomb, sweet to the soul and healing to the bones" (Proverbs 16:24). They will heal you *and* others. Ah, but pleasant words can only come from a heart where good fruit grows.

One more thing. God wants you to produce fruit you can eat. Then you will have no problem offering it to others—or to God, who longs to sample our fruit on a regular basis. Remember, trees don't get to choose where they are planted. Their seed is in the hand of the gardener who knows best, but they produce fruit anyway because it is their nature. The soil of your circumstances may not exactly be to your liking, but it should not hinder your ability to yield an inviting, luscious crop.

Finally, if you are a Christian, your connection to the True Vine should put it in your nature to produce good fruit. Jesus said, "I am the vine; you are the branches. If a man remains in me and I in him, he will bear much fruit; apart from me you can do nothing" (John 15:5). This ability to bear fruit has nothing to do with your circumstances. It has everything to do with your relationship to God. The closer we are to Him, the sweeter our fruit, because everything we do will be ripened by love. He is not impressed with you looking your religious best. He wants to sample your fruit to see if you taste like Him. He comes looking to see if He can use what you have to feed others. This is His ultimate goal.

So don't just *bloom*. Bear fruit and flourish!

➤ LOOKING INWARD ◄

- What does your garden look like?
- What weeds need to be uprooted and discarded?
- In what ways has your fruit affected others?
- What fruit do you produce at work?
- Are you ready for God to taste your fruit?
- What would you like to grow more of in your garden?

➤ LOOKING UPWARD ◄

"But the fruit of the Spirit is love, joy, peace, patience, kindness, goodness, faithfulness, gentleness and self-control. Against such things there is no law" (Galatians 5:22-23).

FIGHT YOUR REAL ENEMY

By now you know there is no quick fix for most situations. Only new strength to see you through. God is not into ending our troubles over-night. He knows that would rob us of the precious opportunity to grow greater character. He is not enlisting wimps into the kingdom of God. He is looking for fighters. But not just any old fighters. He is looking for champions who will stand and not be bowed by opposition. Who have been seasoned by going through the paces of everyday life and the various changes it takes us through.

Life is a battle. We are in a war. Not a war with people. A war between good and evil. The struggle is real. We must learn how to fight. In days of old, God left certain enemy nations in the land in order to teach warfare to the generation of Israelites who had no experience in battle (Judges 3:2). God wants you to know how to fight the real enemy—Satan—when he assaults you.

> Put on the full armor of God, so that when the day of evil comes,
> you may be able to stand your ground, and after you have done
> everything, to stand. Stand firm then, with the belt of truth buckled
> around your waist, with the breastplate of righteousness in place,
> and with your feet fitted with the readiness that comes from the
> gospel of peace. In addition to all this, take up the shield of faith,
> with which you can extinguish all the flaming arrows of the evil
> one. Take the helmet of salvation and the sword of the Spirit, which
> is the word of God. And pray in the Spirit on all occasions with all
> kinds of prayers and requests. With this in mind, be alert and
> always keep on praying for all the saints. (Ephesians 6:13-18)

Stand firm. God is on your side. While the enemy aims at your weaknesses in order to exploit you, God focuses on your weaknesses in order to strengthen you. Though you may suffer, know and believe that no weapon the enemy has created to defeat you will be successful.

As you move forward to claim greater happiness, deeper fulfillment, mightier achievements, you will have to fight. The enemy will not give up new territory without a fight. Press your way, as the old saints say, toward the victory. You can make it.

Jesus, knowing the joy that was before Him, endured the cross, not even considering the shame associated with such a humiliating death, in order to reach His final destination. Afterward, He sat down at the right hand of God, having paid the price to redeem His beloved bride—us. Jesus made it. But not without a fight. (See Hebrews 12:2-4.)

Sometimes the fight is with the enemy of our souls. Sometimes it is with ourselves as we struggle to loose ourselves from the things that weigh us down and keep us from moving forward. In either case, God challenges us to greater heights in our knowledge of Him and deeper levels of sacrifice so that He can reward us with blessings beyond our imagination. If we persevere, we will prevail and take hold of the prize.

Do you feel yourself growing weary? Lift up your head and your hands to God. He is faithful to send help. Moses held his hands above his head as the battle raged between the Israelites and their enemy Amalek. Whenever Moses grew weary and dropped his hands, the enemy would begin to win. When he lifted his hands, the Israelites would begin to win again. Finally Aaron and Hur stood beside Moses and supported his arms until the Israelites' enemy was finally defeated at sundown. Aaron, a Levite priest, and Hur, from the tribe of Judah, symbolize prayer and praise. Prayer and praise will keep you connected to the Source of your help so He can see you through.

Jesus, God's Son, will not turn His back on you while you are fighting. He will light the way to your victory. He will not steer you away from the fight, but He will lead you through it. Do not draw back in fear.

Embrace your suffering, mount your struggle, and ride it like an adventur-
ous surfer who knows the wave will break and move you toward the shore
where rest awaits you.

➤ LOOKING INWARD ◄

- Whom have you targeted as the enemy in your situation?
- How much control do they really have over your situation?
- How much control have you given to them?
- Are you able to look beyond them and see other forces at work?
- In what ways will you change your battle strategy in light of this
  new information? What internal weapons will you use?

➤ LOOKING UPWARD ◄

"For our struggle is not against flesh and blood, but against the rulers,
against the authorities, against the powers of this dark world and against
the spiritual forces of evil in the heavenly realms" (Ephesians 6:12).

Stay Ahead of the Game

How do you stay ahead of life and its drama? By having a few basic facts firmly entrenched in your understanding. This makes you an offensive player versus a defensive end in the game of life. Trust me, a little understanding can go a long way. Therefore, get as much as you can.

What should you understand? Several things. Let's take them one by one.

Fact number one. You have an enemy. It is not God. It is Satan. The great liar and deceiver. The accuser of us all. Don't be surprised. Don't go into denial. He will do his thing whether you acknowledge him or not. Christian or not, you have an enemy. God warns us of this in Genesis 3:15. Study your opponent. Know his agenda. The enemy of your soul is bent on three goals: steal, kill, and destroy. Basically, he wants to wreak havoc in your world. He wants you to blame God and give up the faith. Don't fall for it. His bark is worse than his bite.

Fact number two. Because of the first fact, trouble will come. This should not be a surprise. Christian or not, you will endure trials. As a Christian you might, in fact, have a few more, simply because you have stirred up the enemy's wrath by switching sides. Find your comfort in knowing you're on the right side. Mordecai, Queen Esther's uncle, told his niece not to think she would be exempt from the enemy's plans just because she lived in the king's palace. There is no way around trouble, but there is a way *through* it. I will repeat this simply because it is worth repeating. Pain is inevitable; misery is optional. Decide what your frame of mind will be when the plot thickens in your life. Will you press the pause button or let the story play out, expecting a good ending? The choice is up to you. Yes, you *do* have a choice in the matter.

Fact number three. You have an advocate. Someone on your side. It is none other than God Himself. Jesus is the only One who has gotten the victory over your enemy, Satan. He will fight with you and defend you. Stick close. Heed His instructions, and you will win too. Life may have other plans for you, but so does God. Bigger and better ones. And He is determined to have His way. While He may not prevent your troubles, He most certainly will make a way out for you that brings you closer to the fulfillment of His plan.

Fact number four. God "does not willingly bring affliction or grief to the children of men" (Lamentations 3:33). But He does *use* our troubles. *Use them for what?* you ask. To teach us obedience. To build our faith. To strengthen us. To stretch us. To move us to a place of greater blessing. To glorify Himself in *your life.* To prove to you that He is all He promised He would be. *Well, that's a cruel way to get my attention,* you might think. Not so. It would be far more cruel for Him to allow you to go through life without giving you a true revelation of His character. To withhold this from you would be to make Him like a lover who never shows you the same considerations he or she has showered on others. You would feel robbed of the true experience of enjoying this person.

If you never get to know the power of God, you will remain fruitless no matter how much you achieve materially. Fruitless. That means lacking joy and peace, unable to give or accept true love, unable to be gentle and kind when others are being unlovely, and unable to be patient with the weaknesses of others. You will find it hard to appreciate the basic goodness of life or master self-control over your cravings. Others will control your level of joy. Things will become obsessions. You will become driven. Even if you don't know what you're driving toward.

Have you ever seen the misery of those who accumulate much, yet lack inner peace and contentment? It makes you wonder what life is all about. Why bother with accumulation if your soul cannot be satisfied? If you spend your life forever pursuing the missing piece?

Without a relationship with God, you wouldn't recognize the missing piece if you bumped right into it—kingdom living. What exactly does that mean? It means right standing with God that gives us a peace beyond understanding and a joy that no trial or problem in this world can take away. How is that possible? Because His Spirit dwells in people who have a relationship with Him, and His Spirit keeps us grounded no matter what is going on. We are grounded in the knowledge that God Himself will give us victory as we surrender to Him ourselves and all that we hold dear.

This is the gentle peace and beauty we see in those who have suffered loss and been completely broken. You can almost smell the sweetness of their countenance. Grace exudes from their pores. A peace that provokes you to jealousy. That is the result of suffering that leads to utter brokenness. It kills everything that rises up in defiance against the will of God, and it leaves something in its wake that is intangible, yet felt by all. That is the power and beauty of true brokenness.

Nothing greater can be required of a person than what God required of His own Son. Jesus learned obedience by the things He suffered. Though He was destined to be Savior and Lord, His life as a man was not exempt from trouble. You name it, He went through it, but He was not unnerved by any of it. Why not? Because He was not relying on His own power; He was connected to the Father. He was secure, and He did not fear His future.

God wants us to abandon the concept of being minigods in and of ourselves and instead choose to embrace a close and personal connection to Him. He wants us not just to be His sons and daughters, but to actually grow to look like Him as well. Inwardly and outwardly. What does God look like? He is unadulterated love manifested through suffering and being broken for our sakes, yet standing unbowed, strengthened by the experience. Both fierce and beautiful to behold, overcoming in spite of it all.

There you have it. Suffering is not a punishment. It is not a sign of weakness or inability on our part. It is, very simply put, a challenge to us. Will we merely reach for God or will we stretch to touch Him? The woman with the issue of blood—her story is told in Matthew 9:20-22—

had suffered for twelve years and no longer cared what anyone thought. (Bleeding women were considered unclean and untouchable, and subject to ostracism.) She did not care about what was considered proper. She only knew one thing: *I must touch Jesus. If I could just reach the hem of His garment, it would be enough for me.* And when she did, she was healed.

Whether we are victims of our own bad choices, victims of the sins of other people, or simply citizens in a world that has lost touch with God and His ways, His reason for allowing suffering is the same: He wants us to look up. To reach out for relationship with Him. Why? Because He knows that life happens. With all its jolts and disappointments. We need Him in order to keep standing when life is falling down around us. And we must be willing to admit it.

God is almighty, and He is good. He is faithful to the end, though He allows us to write our own stories by the choices we make. In the end, we who are in relationship with God will overcome. Our stories will be about glorious victories in spite of what life brings us, because we have grasped the reality of Christ's blood, which was shed for us in order to give us relationship with God and overcoming power in life. And that is good.

No longer do we have to fear touching God, as did people of the Old Testament whose sin (like ours) separated them from God. Through Jesus, we now have unfettered access to the Holy One. He wants to help us, but He will not push Himself upon us. We must cast down our pride and be willing to voice our need for a Savior. For a relationship with God. At the end of the day, we come full circle to the reason for suffering: It magnifies our need for relationship with God.

If you already have a relationship with God, then take your cue. Draw closer. If you don't have a relationship with God, now is the time. What better day to end the struggle? If you've had a relationship with God but allowed it to drift south while you were trying to solve your own problems or were being needlessly angry with Him, now is the time to start over. What better moment than now to start anew? Either way, today is your day. Let's pray together:

Dear heavenly Father, I stand before You greatly in need of Your help. I have struggled and wrestled with my own life, in my own strength, long enough. I am unable to find solutions to my problems, to fill the gaping void in my life. I am in need of wisdom, solace, a Redeemer. I fully understand that I am a sinner in need of grace and that You have paid the price for my failings with the blood of Your own Son. I ask that You forgive my sin; that You wash me, cleanse me, and make me acceptable in Your sight. I want to be in right relationship with You. Jesus, I accept the payment You made for my salvation, and I ask You to become my Savior and Lord. I believe in my heart and now confess with my mouth that You are indeed Lord. I can no longer chart my own course. I willingly choose to yield to Your direction. I now release and place all my burdens in Your hands, and I place my trust in You. Grant me wisdom and the strength to follow your leading. In Jesus' name I pray. Amen.

There. Now don't you feel better already? I would really like to know whether you prayed this prayer so that I can rejoice with you. Please write to me at either of the following addresses:

HeartWing Ministries
P.O. Box 11052
Chicago, IL 60611

heartwingmin@yahoo.com
or log on to www.heartwing.org

Above all else remember: No matter what you feel you've lost, keep the faith. You are not alone!

Rest assured:

Life happens…

Death happens…

Then life begins again.

Bible Characters
Referenced in This Book

If you want to study this person in more detail:	See these chapters of *Get Over It and On With It:*	And these Bible passages:
Abigail	"When Life Robs Your Peace," 24, 25, 26, 27, 28	1 Samuel 25:2-44; 2 Samuel 17:25
David	"When Life Robs Your Peace, " 3, 8, 12, 14, 15, 25, 26, 27, 28	1 Samuel 16; 1Kings 2:12; 1 Chronicles 11–29; Matthew 1:1,6,17
Elijah	"When Life Knocks the Wind Out of You, " 1, 2, 3, 5, 6, 11, 19, 29, 31, 35, 38	1 Kings 17–19; 2 Kings 1:1–2:18; Malachi 4:5; Matthew 17:3,10; Mark 9:12-13; John 1:21
Job	"When Life Assaults Your Faith," 4, 9, 12, 13, 14, 16, 18, 22, 23	The Book of Job; James 5:11
Joseph	"When Life Destroys Your Dreams," 7, 14, 17, 18, 20, 21, 22, 23, 32, 33, 35, 36	Genesis 37:1–50:26; Acts 7:9-18; Hebrews 11:22
Ruth	"When Life Takes What Is Dear," 29, 30, 31, 34, 37, 38, 39, 40, 41	The Book of Ruth